1996 SWARTHMORE LECTURE

BEYOND THE SPIRIT OF THE AGE

Quaker social responsibility at the end of the twentieth century

JONATHAN DALE

QUAKER HOME SERVICE
LONDON

F50

First published May 1996 by
QUAKER HOME SERVICE
Friends House
Euston Road
London NW1 2BJ

ISBN 0-85245-282-9

Cover photograph by John Noble

PREFACE

The Swarthmore Lectureship was established by the Woodbrooke Extension Committee at a meeting on the 9th December 1907: the minute of the Committee provided for an 'annual lecture on some subject relating to the message and work of the Society of Friends'. The name 'Swarthmore' was chosen in memory of the home of George and Margaret Fox, which was always open to the earnest seeker after Truth, and from which loving words of sympathy and substantial material help were sent to fellow workers.

The lectureship has a twofold purpose: first, to interpret to the members of the Religious Society of Friends their message and mission; secondly, to bring before the public the spirit, the aims and fundamental principles of Friends. The lecturers alone are responsible for any opinions expressed.

The lectureship provides both for the publication of a book and for the delivery of a lecture, the latter usually at the time of assembly of the Yearly Meeting of the Religious Society of Friends (Quakers) in Britain. A lecture related to the present book was delivered at Friends House, Euston Road, London, on the evening of the 4th May 1996.

ACKNOWLEDGMENTS

I take this opportunity of thanking Pam Lunn and Christopher Holdsworth for their stimulation and encouragement. Most of all Emily has been a constant source of reassurance, even when I have neglected the cooking and cleaning. This book also owes something to my three children, Med, Gareth and Branwen who have all striven to undermine my complacency and my caution. But this book could not have been written without the communities which made me what I am: St. Andrew's Meeting, Quaker Social Responsibility & Education's Central Committee and the people of Guardbridge, Wythenshawe and Ordsall. I owe them much that money cannot buy.

CONTENTS

INTRODUCTION

The core of the Quaker tradition is a way of inward seeking which leads to outward acts of integrity and service. Friends are most in the Spirit when they stand at the crossing point of the inward and the outward life. And that is the intersection at which we find community.

Parker J. Palmer[1]

Beyond Realism

First we must dream. Nothing is harder. Just try to engage from cold in an exercise to discern the social evils which are today's equivalents of slavery! Dreaming has to break through the constantly reinforced assumption that 'There Is No Alternative'. Political discourse has been largely reduced to a narrow space. Realism is all. Dreaming beyond those boundaries, for politicians, is subject to severe punishment at the hands of the media and the people.

The churches have become one of the places where dreaming is kept alive. They have sometimes been distorted into defending the status quo but their birthright, our birthright, is prophecy and the kingdom. In the Bible, dreaming keeps alive God's hope for 'His' people and for all of us. But the dream has to start, as it does in the Old Testament, with the outright refusal of an unjust and idolatrous reality. Longer term solutions do not come fully formed. They emerge in the energy of outrage at the evils that surround us. Contemplation is about seeing things as they really - ultimately - are. What can we see?

We see huge and deepening inequalities of income, wealth, health, education and opportunity within our own nations. 'Realism' tells us - misleadingly - both that these inequalities are inevitable and that poverty will disappear as the poor come to benefit from the spending of the rich. Reform orientated politicians daringly propose limited adjustments. Is that enough? Our dream is of a much more radical equality, a community of people equal in dignity and much more equal in wealth and in the power and opportunity associated with it.

If that is true for this country, how can we not apply it internationally, where inequalities are massively greater again and the gap between wealthiest and poorest nations grows all the time. The poorest 50 nations with 25% of the world's population have just 2% of its income. 'Realism' says that the global market is the means to growth which will benefit all; if some lose out they can be helped by special measures. But we see millions of people exploited in this market, where the power of capital is vastly greater than the power of labour. We are using their time, their health, their well-being, often to satisfy whims more than needs. Our dream of world-wide equality is inescapable and yet awesome in its implicit demands on us.

We see a world threatened by environmental impoverishment, if not ruin. Species are being destroyed in their thousands as habitats are decimated. Forests are felled indiscriminately and fishing areas are on the brink of exhaustion. We have polluted the air and are destroying the ozone layer with potentially devastating consequences. And all this when only a small part of the world's population is at an advanced level of material development. The effect of achieving material equality at current levels can hardly be contemplated. We seem trapped in a mind-set which stops us taking timely preventative actions. We risk our health by prioritising speed, convenience and greater consumption over it. As Friends we have failed sufficiently to develop our testimonies in this direction to take action before it is forced on us by government or by catastrophe. We lament globally but carry on individually as if we were helpless.

We see also deep flaws in our democratic system. Friends' faith in democracy a century ago has not been realised. Economic power is more concentrated rather than less. Governmental power remains strongly centralised and as unaccountable as ever

2

in crucial respects. Social power is also still narrowly centred - in the wealthy-public-school-and- 'Oxbridge-educated' class. The culture of citizenship is debased - in some ways political debate is cruder than it was in the generation after the Manchester Conference. The politicisation and commercialisation of the civil and public services have damaged their ethos. Deceit of the public, as well as of parliament, has been exposed by the Scott enquiry and political life is widely seen as venal and sordid. The culture of honest democratic debate remains to be created.

In such a world the individualistic struggle for success, power, or sheer survival mushrooms into different forms of anti-social behaviour. On the one hand the 'legitimate' greed of the share options of the privatised utilities; on the other crime and vandalism. The individual responds by retreating into his or her beleaguered private space, leaving public space as a menacing sort of no person's land ruled in different ways by gangs of young males of varying ages from three upwards. We cannot be surprised at the violence of young people in a divided society which has little use or respect for them. How, then, can we witness to our dream of true community, where all are valued, where no-one needs to resort to the law of the jungle to find fulfilment?

All these features of contemporary society are visible accompaniments of life in areas such as Ordsall, where I now live. The inequality and injustice surfaces at every turn: in the women who run the New Barracks Housing Co-op with dedication and ability but cannot get a paid job other than as cleaners; in the older people who are almost all in very poor health by the time they're sixty; in the parents working split shifts to provide for the children they scarcely have time for. As for democracy, little is expected of it. The experience here is of being controlled by the powers that be; of one's voice being ignored; of knocking one's head against a brick wall. The environment is harsh and in many ways harmful: the area is surrounded by major roads; the noise is continuous and the air quality is often very poor - asthma is almost the norm.

Anxiety or violence are never far away: in the debt problems that mount as soon as wages drop and the omnipresent fear of redundancy; in the health problems in young and old; in the strain of family relationships; the abuse of toddlers; the doors kicked in; the police raids; the armed robberies; the petrol bombing. All this is the fall-out from the dominant world's worship of success, wealth and power. Such places are kept out of sight and out of mind until the riot headlines remind us. It is increasingly a form of segregation.

So, this is our situation: after centuries of social progress, the development of democracy and the welfare state, and the generation of massive levels of individual and social wealth, we have lost confidence in our ability to create a good and just social order. Suicide rates, mental illness, fear of violence, incidence of physical and sexual abuse, breakdowns of family relationships and acts of vandalism figure amongst the indicators of the diseased social body. We live with unacceptable levels of fear; in some urban areas like Ordsall most adults are afraid to remonstrate with anyone of any age doing anything which they shouldn't. Either their windows will be broken, or their bones. For some, these things are daily dilemmas. If an inventor of Quakerism was looking for a site to test it this is the sort of place s/he would choose.

As the inequality and injustice intensifies, so the demand for harsher methods of social control augments. The police are armed with new weapons year by year; sentences are increased; more prisons are built. We can sense the model of the United States as our destination, where in excess of one million people are incarcerated.

It is in this situation that Friends must choose where Britain Yearly Meeting (BYM) stands. We can stay silent in the face of such blatant injustices as the Poll Tax. We can adopt the position of those Friends who opposed the Yearly Meeting's Poverty Statement in 1987 and keep right out of the political arena. We can give up on corporate witness on the grounds that we will never agree. We can hole up in the comfortable world of a spirituality of moods and relationships. But, if we do so, our opt-out means supporting the status quo with all the injustice and distress which I have pointed to. It means acknowledging that we have nothing to say as a Religious Society.

The purpose of this lecture is to exhort Friends to match the reality of our social disorder with a robust spiritual response, a readiness to go beyond the voices which counsel extreme caution or withdrawal. Our spiritual reality will be known by our ability to grapple with the forces in society which have weakened community, distorted truth and corrupted the potential for love. We cannot surely keep silence in the face of so much misery. Rather we should seek ways of bringing our vision of the good society much more actively into the political arena.

*   *   *

This, then, is a world in which metaphorically nails continue to be driven into the bodies and minds of many. I have not included as many voices as I would have liked from the 'sharp end'. We need to hear them because it is the experience of oppression that creates the fullest understanding of liberation. But I want you to hear this voice, the voice of a man who was almost destroyed by the system which dealt him out the experience of unemployment. His story, albeit with greater intensity and a happier ending, is the story of many people. I heard it at a conference I had organised when I worked for Church Action on Poverty. It was spoken into a silent Sunday morning meeting for reflection, when we really listened to each other's pains and joys. It was not a Meeting for Worship. Yet it was the most powerful Meeting for Worship I have ever experienced.[2] The spirit was with us; listen to it:

D:
Well mine's a story of long-term unemployment since 1984. And before that, in the late 70s, I was redundant twice in the construction industry. In 1984 I got a job in the Redcar works

5

relining the furnaces. I'd been out of work for about four months. When I was on the night shift on my second week, I was stiffening up, because I wasn't used to heavy work. I used to rub myself with Fiery Jack and by two o'clock in the morning I was sweating and stinking of this Fiery Jack. I thought it was just me muscles. But it wasn't... it was Chronic Lumbardiscolesion. I started to seize up [...].

Anyway, I seized up completely, like, and I lay on the bedroom floor for a fortnight till I eased off; but this pain went on and on; then, finally, they put me on invalidity benefit. I was on sick and invalidity benefit for about fourteen months.

In that time I started to suffer from anxiety; I was really concerned about where me life was going, what was going to happen to me and me family. Me dignity was going, and me self-respect; and there was the frustration of not knowing what to do. I was completely slowed down and I was walking like an old man ... so I decided to get meself active, mobile, like, and I went out and started picking up pieces of wood. I've a three by four foot shed in the back of me garden, so I decided to do some carving. So I said, 'Lass, get me some carving tools out of the Catalogue, will you.' She said: 'Right, I'll get you some' [...] Because I wanted to keep occupied. Before, I was running to the library reading all the time, and I think this brought the anxiety on, 'cos I'd sit for hours [...]reading books, on history and all sorts; and I used to get cold sweats and hot sweats and palpitations. It was that bad, I used to run outside and strip me shirt and vest off, or run upstairs and lay flat on the bedroom floor - it felt like me heart was coming out of me chest. And that's what the doctor said it was - severe anxiety due to the long-term unemployment situation, which was getting on top of me, pressing me further and further down.

So I turned to prayer. And I've never prayed so much in me life as I did them first few years ... the pain of being out of work, the physical suffering and the mental pain on top of that. Anyway I started doing these carvings. I got that involved, carried away by these carvings - two of our Lord, one of the crucifix and one of the crown of thorns - I was over the moon with it ... I was in this three foot by four foot shed for a couple of days with this manky wood, shaping it into what I wanted it to be ... and it turned out exactly what I wanted it to be.

And, from there, D was introduced to the voluntary sector via the MSC's Community Programme. Although he never got a 'proper' paid job again he recovered his dignity in helping others.

The way of the world deals with this horror in two ways. Either it lays all the blame on the 'victim', claiming that there is always work for those prepared to look for it. Or it treats them as the unfortunate casualties of economic development which produces prosperity for the rest. That argument echoes seductively in the recesses of our minds. Yet, can we so easily discount such suffering and turn a blind eye to such injustice? Better by far to recognise that the suffering is systematic; that is to say that society has chosen not to share more equally either the goods or the pain that the system creates.

I use the term 'society' advisedly. We cannot lay all the blame on government. Governments certainly play an important role and I shall show how powerfully they can act in the interests of the rich. They are not, however, completely free agents. They cannot lose touch completely with public opinion. Public opinion needs to be addressed.

Currently politicians assume that public opinion will not support any major redistribution of wealth nor any significant increase in taxation to meet the needs of those who are homeless or on very low benefits; it clamours for a punitive approach to penal policy. And so on. Can we stand aside from these debates as though they do not engage our testimonies?

If the world proclaims the impossibility of greater justice nationally or internationally, we must dissent. Our social arrangements today are not God's final word. Our faith values - truth, equality, simplicity, peace, community - are a judgement on the world as it is and our guides to the world as it must become. Can we withhold those values from the public debate? The distinctive contribution to the world that the Society of Friends is best fitted to make at this time is this: a whole-hearted recognition that our corporate influence is needed in the public realm where the kingdom of God is always being built or destroyed.

*   *   *

Scope and Plan

In this lecture I try to diagnose the state of Quaker social witness in Great Britain in the last decade of the twentieth century. The central question I address is the following: How far should the dominant social and political structures and values in the United Kingdom command our Quaker assent or dissent? Such a large question needs to be approached in a broad context. So I have ranged widely over our beliefs, trying to uncover some of the elements in the contemporary or recent climate of ideas which underlie our attitudes to social issues.

By choosing to focus on the preconditions for effective social witness I am unable to do justice to other vital approaches. Readers will find less detailed analysis of social issues than they might expect. Even though I focus on issues of social justice in Great Britain I have not found space for close discussion of poverty, housing problems, unemployment and the like. I must simply hope that Friends are well enough informed. I have found even less space for the democratic deficit, the ecological crisis and the global dimension of injustice, each of which is enormously important. Much of my argument can be easily adapted and applied to these fields and I trust will be. As for new directions and solutions, all I have been able to do is offer a few brief sketches.

The weight of my argument is directed more towards freeing our Society of Friends to become itself a more effective agent in the generation of the vision of a new society and in the practical transformation of the old.

I make no claim to a methodical examination of the historical background to these issues. However, I did, by chance, find myself reading almost all the Swarthmore Lectures up to 1950. I have quoted extensively from them to provide some historical depth; many of the most important points have already been made. But, what has changed decisively is our assessment of the direction of change. We have lost faith in progress. That loss of faith decisively alters the context of our social witness.

After this introduction, the book begins with a consideration of the relationship of faith and action, or rather faith-in action. Then, through the key concepts of relativism, secularism and individualism, I look at how cultural history has affected the expression of our faith and its potential for social witness. I examine next inequality, consumerism and the capitalist economic structure as contemporary challenges to our faith. Chapter Five takes up Margaret Heathfield's theme of how we envisage our corporate identity[3] and I conclude with some signs of hope, within both BYM and wider British society.

But first, I offer an account of the standpoints from which this book is written, as a help to the reader.

My Understanding of Faith

I am one of those Friends who believe that the light within is also beyond. If it were *only* within, I would wonder how it could transcend death. And, if it was not transcendent in that sense, how could it be more than the subjectively human. So my faith is based on a conviction that there is a beyond in our midst which brings the ultimate into our day-to-day world. There is something beyond mere opinion, something which partakes of absolute truth and perfect love.

Within us there is that which is drawn towards this truth and love which I have come to call God, a term which I have had to relearn how to use. For a long time I contemplated the good, being unable to name God. I focused on the immanence of truth and love; I spoke of the ground of our being. My religion seemed an aspect of humankind as it is, a way of looking at its deepest potentialities. I stressed the naturalness of religion.

Later, when I came, slowly, to name God, God was still a purpose, a spirit, which I could not think of as personal. When I understood that love cannot be impersonal and that, therefore, in some mysterious way, God must be personal I reached the point where I am now. God is personal but also ultimate. Immanent but also transcendent. Unchanging but progressively revealed. Even if we can never know God's will absolutely because we live in the world of relativities, I believe that we are informed by the absolutes of Truth and Love which are of God. Our glimpses and interpretations of God are coloured by our subjectivity, but God is not. God is, I believe, real, not just what we have invented for our comfort.

I have not mentioned Jesus. My faith has not been explicitly derived from that amazing story. It has emerged in reflection and experience within a framework of natural religion. I might not call myself a Christian. And, yet, I acknowledge that almost all the elements of my faith are marked by the Old or the New Testaments: the strong themes of the God of justice in the Old Testament, a God speaking to a people in both anger and hope through 'His' prophets; the castigation of idolatry, the worship of false gods, which is so relevant to our world; and, from the New Testament, the releasing promise of forgiveness and the story of sacrificial love, of a defeat which is transformed into victory because life has been lived from within God's spirit. Over that, death has no dominion.

In short I am one of those who were tempted by the existentialist view of the individual, free to invent her or his own values in a world without pre-existing ones; but who has come to believe that the individual cannot be the origin of value. I am one of those who found orthodox religious language hollow and have begun to reappropriate it. Now, almost all the language that I discarded is needed to express what my spiritual experience has brought to me.

My Political Understanding of Faith

Equality was in the air I breathed in my Quaker upbringing. I have never doubted that the implications of our testimony to equality are real: no subject peoples abroad; no exploited class at home; no oppressed gender. To believe in that of God in everyone is not a passive description it is a Quaker Commandment. I take for granted that any concentration of power, including the concentration of financial power under capitalism, destroys equality. I have been a member of the Labour Party for over thirty years.

However, this book is situated beyond the current lines of party politics. No Party can afford to embody what I suggest Friends should stand for. This prompts a reflection which I believe will be relevant to many Friends.

It centres on principle and compromise. Some Friends suggest that compromise is wicked. I take a different view. Individually one may aspire to live out a pure principle, such as pacifism - though in practice it is not easy to avoid all compromise, for example, in bringing up children, or relying on police protection, armed if necessary. However, in the political realm, compromise is both inevitable and necessary. Our 'principles' are mixed in with the principles and the self-interest of millions of other people: teetotallers might believe that alcohol should be banned but agree that it should not be part of the political programme of their party because such a ban has little support in the population at large. That ought not to be controversial.

This book essentially takes a prophetic approach and asks the question whether society as it is, is compatible with our faith. I hope Friends can agree that it is perfectly honest to operate politically both towards the distant horizon and to seek short-term goals. That's why I remain a member of the Labour Party, even though I am very critical of its conservative cautiousness. It seems to me, for the moment, the best-placed mechanism for achieving some of the goals that fall within the major testimonies of the Society. And it retains some connection with the history of organised labour, which the Society of Friends, as an institution, has lacked to its loss.

My Class Standpoint

I have lived in the culture of the professional middle class all my life. *The News Chronicle* and later *The Guardian*. I spent twenty years in university teaching. There is nothing wrong with that standpoint, except its tendency to cut you off. All standpoints inevitably do.

I have been working as a community worker in exploited urban environments for the last twelve years and Emily and I now live in an almost entirely working class part of Salford. I do not pretend that my standpoint is the same as those I live and work amongst, despite our move to share aspects of the same vantage point - the Barracks Estate. Nonetheless I am closer to it. However we do it, we need to share something of what poverty and marginalisation mean if our faith is to be real. If we do, we become aware that power is unequal and that justice has always been won through struggle. And that one perennial dimension of social struggle is the class struggle, even if the definition of the classes may change.

Both Problem and Solution

Truth is the starting point for spiritual growth, in social faithfulness as in other ways. So it would be dishonest of me to write about concepts like discipleship, testimony and faith-through-action, without giving some account of my own material situation. We always need to ask ourselves in what ways we add to exploitation and inequality and in what ways we alleviate it. Our 'balance sheets' will cover everything: personal relationships, attitudes, values, lifestyle, use of time and resources. Some of us will contribute more than others to one side or the other of the equation, but it is our fundamental solidarity that we all figure on both.

What I write may suggest that I live a life in conformity with my proclaimed beliefs. I need to make it abundantly clear that I do not. This book is written as part of my continuing struggle. An unfinished struggle, in particular, to lessen my dependence on material security. I hope and believe that openness to ourselves and others about our spiritual state fosters preparedness to change. Let me illustrate these points on the subjects of housing and, more painfully, money.

I grew up in a simple and comfortable suburban semi-detached home. For two years after my degree and marriage, Emily and I lived in basic private rented accommodation in Blackburn. Then I took a lecturing job in St Andrews and we fell in love with an old cottage, the Poffle, with a cottage attached and an acre of land - £3,200. The empty cottage was condemned and seen as a liability; the development potential of the land was not considered at all. We spent twenty years there.

Conditions changed. The condemned cottage became eligible for an improvement grant. We also had two improvement grants for our main cottage, giving us new kitchen, central heating, damp proof course etc. Later, we experimented with a two-family community, until it became clear that it was not equally creative for all four adults.

Eventually I felt called to a different life and we had to face the shock of leaving our abundant, if untidy paradise. We sold each cottage separately and the land went for two building plots, raising £61,000 in all. We bought a large house in a 'favoured' area of Manchester for £41,000. The £10,000 for the land was clearly a windfall gain and we gave the money away. At least another £10,000 represented the improvements which society in general had paid me to make, although our combined earnings were way above the average. We were being subsidised by taxation, including tax payments by people much worse off than us. We were astonished not to have to repay anything.

Those special circumstances were not, of course, the only way in which our housing affluence was being subsidised. Like most house purchasers we benefited from Mortgage Interest Tax Relief. When I came to work in Ordsall my housing subsidy was greater than most of those with whom I was working. I knew it was a scandalous injustice. For some years it was part of my calculation in contributing to the Monthly Meeting's Poverty Action Fund. Not a donation but a reparation.

For six years I cycled across Manchester into inner city Salford to work. From the Didsbury villas and the opulent trees to the glass-strewn roads and graffiti-scrawled walls of Ordsall. Two worlds. What did it mean to live in one and visit the other to work? In the end, after much resistance in ourselves, we had to move to Ordsall and share more parts of our life with some of those who are being hardest hit by the policies which have widened the gulf between the well-off and the poor. Selling for £100,000, we bought for £36,000, a house which might be impossible to sell, unless at a big loss. If so, so be it. It would certainly be our turn.

Reflecting on that story it is self evident that our housing choices, up to our latest move, have been exercises in the power that comes with financial opportunity, the power to take for ourselves what we wanted. The story of the unjust distribution of housing opportunities can be seen in our lives. Friends have long recognised that employment choice needs to be faced as a spiritual opportunity, I see no reason why housing choice should be any different.

I am a case study of middle class advantage more broadly - in relation to money - the great taboo amongst Friends. How can I explain our having a quarter of a million pounds. I can't really believe it myself. How has it come about?

Not largely by inheritance. My great-grandfather's fortune had largely been spent before my generation. We have had significant sums from parents, but not on this scale. I inherited £14,000 from my mother but gave it away. Emily has received £23,000 from her father. I have recently been given £12,000 by mine, after foregoing another £25,000 in favour of charities.

Our current earned income has contributed significantly. Neither of us, however, has ever earned £20,000 a year and I gave up my lecturing post and took a 50% drop in salary as a community worker. I now work half-time by choice so that my time is available for other things. However, combined earnings of £26,000, are more than enough in the eyes of simplicity or sufficiency. Our standard of living is probably between two and three times higher than the Income Support level after housing costs. We want for nothing.

So, where does the £250,000 come from? There are two main mechanisms. I left the university through a voluntary severance arrangement which paid me a £35,000 lump sum to replace probable loss of earnings and pension rights. That has grown to some £100,000 now. Trading down twice in the housing market has added £10,000 in 1984 and £69,000 in 1994 - at current values around another £100,000. My wealth has become more visible as it is no longer in the form of housing and pension rights.

You see here the basis of middle class material security, in housing, pension rights or invested cash - or, indeed all three. And the many measures which help the better off more than the poor are revealed. Objectively, my politics run the risk of being inflected towards my self-interest. Even if I avoid that danger I am likely to be too insulated from the experience of those who are on society's margins to make their cause my own - with passion.

I am certainly part of the problem as well as striving to assist solutions, as are we all. Over the years I have become clearer about my housing choice; with my? money, it is still an unresolved skirmish between the fragments of myself that speak different languages. The language of material security and that other language of trust in God.

I do believe that Friends need to become as open on matters of financial stewardship as they have in terms of sexuality. We cannot be honest about our social responsibility unless we are honest about the very material ways in which we express it before we even open our mouths. Can we believe enough in the light that is both truth and also love, to share our secret financial lives without fear? If, despite our incessant invocations of the light, we fail, it can only be because we do not really believe that it will take us as we are, and lead us closer to itself.

A Broad Brush

I ask readers to understand that my approach is to convey the broad thrust of what seems true to me. I know that there will be exceptions to most of the claims I make. I just do not have the space to add all the provisos. I will be trenchant where that seems to me the closest to the truth.

The Critical and the Negative

Some may find me hypercritical of BYM's understanding and practice of social responsibility. Friends often interpret such criticism either as disloyalty or negativity. It is true that, by concentrating on what needs to be changed rather than what can be affirmed, I paint a partial picture. Criticism, even so, is neither disloyal nor negative. I have simply tried to face up to the current situation truthfully. Nor do I see critical argument as gloomy or defeatist. On the contrary, searching for the truth should be exhilarating, new insights reached being a basis for the next forward movement.

I may seem to invoke high standards. I do. They are not mine but derive from our faith, our testimonies. But they should not make anyone feel diminished. Nothing I say should encourage anyone to measure themselves against any human model of faith-in-action. It should rather encourage us all to an ever fuller discipleship in a rich variety of patterns. I simply long for the Society to be, more than it yet has become, a powerhouse of social witness; and for us all to be the encouragement and the inspiration and the goads for each other to that end.

- Chapter 1 -
FAITH AND ACTION

We come to know God first of all by obeying his word.

Thomas Cullinan[1]

For Words without actions are a cheat and kill the comfort of the righteous spirit, so words performed in action do comfort and nourish the spirit thereof.

Gerrard Winstanley[2]

Introduction

'So say, so do' wrote George Fox,[3] Consistency of word and word and word and deed is a challenging inheritance. Nor are these merely secular moral commands: rather they are constitutive of the nature of God, who is pure integrity. Without integrity our spirituality is distorted and our relationship with God clouded. This is the foundation of our Testimony to truth and integrity. For nothing that leads to God is based on the false or hollow.

So, when we say that God is love, the integrity of our claim is known by the degree to which it is fulfilled in our lives. Proof of the pudding of our beliefs lies in what it tastes like to those who eat it. As truth requires the fusion of faith and action, so does love. For, as God is love, there can be no spirituality which is not 'for others'. Moreover, since we believe that there is that of God in everyone, we cannot separate our love of God and of our fellow human beings. Our faith cannot be a secret garden; it is a place in which, in joy and in sorrow, the walls which divide us from our sisters and brothers are taken down.

On the other hand, we inherit the assumption that spirituality is nurtured in solitude. And it may be - also. But we have the word of Thomas Merton that such solitude is a means of deepening relationship, for 'it is deep in solitude that I find the gentleness with which I can truly love my brothers' (*sic*).[4] Even prayer - especially prayer? - which takes us into the deepest inwardness of the real self, is necessarily an opening up of ourselves to the needs of others. As Elisabeth O'Connor expresses it: 'If prayer does not drive us out into some concrete involvement at a point of the world's need, then we must question prayer.'[5] If we could approach prayer in this light we would find it as relevant to the work of Quaker Peace & Service (QPS) and Quaker Social Responsibility & Education (QSRE) as to Quaker Home Service (QHS). I do not think we yet act as though that were so.

The close relationship of faith and action has not always been understood in the same way, but it has remained in the bedrock of Quaker faith since this was laid down. We should celebrate this persistent witness, which time and again turns to the Epistle of James: 'What good is it, my Friends, for someone to say he has faith when his actions do nothing to show it?'[6]

Faith and action

Unity of faith and action has remained a unifying feature of twentieth century Quakerism. We have a precious freedom and strength from not having to argue for this position.[7] We are convinced that faith is not real unless practically embodied. We are also clear that no aspect of life is outside the workings of the spirit of love and of truth.

Yet, for all its centrality and strength, this tradition is being undermined and needs reaffirmation. It is not so much that it is being explicitly attacked; but, indirectly, it is being weakened. I turn now to examine some of these ways in which faith and action are being divorced.

The Separation of Spirituality from the World

The first danger lies in the ready audience for the call to the Society to concentrate on its 'primary task' which is, in Robert Daines' words, to 'look to the spiritual well-being of its adherents'.[8]

In one sense, of course, this statement is true. If by 'spiritual' we understand our total relationship to God, both our inward responsiveness and our outward response to God through our neighbours and the natural world, our spiritual welfare *is* the primary task. But there would also be no need of the statement. An opposition between the 'spiritual' and the rest must be intended: the dualism is clear. If the spiritual is primary, then the rest is secondary and the fusion of faith and action is destroyed.

Such a position is much more common in other churches. Many have had a long tradition of other-worldliness and stress salvation by faith. Indeed much contemporary religious practice can still best be understood in terms of 'privatised spirituality'. By this I mean: an understanding of faith as the private connection between the individual's soul and God; the crucial role of religious observance; and the stress on one's future in the after-life rather than finding in this life the principle of life eternal.

This 'privatised spirituality' is unattractive to most British Friends. However, other aspects of a privatised spirituality may be more of a temptation. The process of secularisation, has driven religion out of large parts of life: out of science, out of morality, out of politics and out of business. Henry Hodgkin shows how the effect of this is to separate religion from life; religion is relegated to 'an ever smaller place in the wide fields of human activity'.[9]

Understood in this way the spiritual is allied to the personal, the private, the experiential and separated from the public world of economic and social life, which is abandoned to the secular world. Kenneth Leech sees the danger: 'religion and spirituality are very much alive, but they have been "privatised", that is, banished to the private sector, to the realm of the personal. Religions have become commodities, and have come to be so restricted in scope that they do not disturb, threaten, or affect the prevailing social order.'[10]

Carl Heath saw the danger signs amongst us some seventy years ago: 'even in the Society of Friends we tend at times to think and act as though some things in corporate and public life had no part [...] in, and no relation to our corporate religious life.'[8] Are we sure that we have not been touched by this powerful process? Are there Friends for whom 'Religion too has become a specialisation and dwells in its own special house'?[12] Do we find traces of this in our Meetings for Worship? Numbers of people who are content to take from them what they need, without much heed to the wider needs of the Meeting or the connection of it all to society at large?

On the one hand, the danger is that spirituality is seen as what happens when we focus inwards. All it then takes is the gradual loss of a sense of God's transcendence for us to find ourselves as the object of our own veneration as we celebrate the inner light in but not beyond ourselves. As John Harvey pointed out: 'if we are less and less consciously worshipping God there is a danger that we may come to an unconscious worship of our own religiosity.' [13]

On the other hand, the corollary of this privatised spirituality is the displacement of religion from its central place in social and economic life. This is particularly clear and well documented in terms of economic activity. It has been vividly analysed by Tawney, as, for example: 'Religion [was] converted from the keystone which holds together the social edifice into one department within it, and the rule of right [was] replaced by economic expediency as the arbiter of policy and the criterion of conduct. From a spiritual being who, in order to survive, must devote a reasonable attention to economic interests, man [sic] seems sometimes to have become an economic animal, who will be prudent nevertheless, if he takes due precautions to secure his spiritual well-being.'[14]

And although Friends started off with some clear guidelines which linked their faith and business practice and these did survive in part, yet a dissociation between business and religious practice in the Society had begun to develop as early as the eighteenth century.[15] Even for Friends who are not actively involved in business, there remains the wider issue of whether we have been persuaded that the economic 'laws' of the market are beyond the reach of faith.

The sweeping impact of secularisation can also be observed in the startling contrast between early twentieth century Friends and ourselves in terms of attitudes to Providence. Friends, at that time, did not always use the term; but, in document after document, there pours through a conviction that God is working through history; that progress is continuing and that our individual lives are part of that wider divine purpose. Faith was more than the story of a personal search; the overcoming of evil was a social as well as an individual necessity - a possibility too. Now, as social pessimism has replaced the social optimism of the first half of the century, we have lost our faith in that grand narrative. Our God has been reduced to a God who can sustain individuals but has lost the power to lead societies ever onwards towards the kingdom of God. The link between our individual story of religious obedience and disobedience and the great narrative of faith has been fractured.

Fortunately other forces have been at work countering this privatising version of Christianity, although it remains a particularly strong influence in the United States. British mainstream churches have experienced an increasing awareness of the implications of faith in terms of social responsibility. Influences at work in this direction have included the impact of liberation theology and of a doctrinaire Conservative Government which created much deeper social problems - in terms of poverty, unemployment and homelessness, for example - than the country has faced for a very long time. The leadership of many churches has spoken out about a wide range of government policies. As the decade went on, the Church of England seems ever less like the Conservative Party at prayer.

However, there has been no comparable movement in Britain Yearly Meeting during that timespan. The Society of Friends has heard voices which looked towards a more radical non-conformity. But, as a whole, the experience of living under sixteen years of the Thatcherite ideological experiment has done little to radicalise the Yearly Meeting as such. Indeed, I have already suggested that there are signs of a drift in the opposite direction. Is a dualistic, privatising spirituality spreading slowly amongst us?

We rarely hear this position elaborated in detail. More usually it is left as the unstated consequence of stances adopted on a whole range of issues: the revaluation of 'being' over 'doing'; the need for a corrective to the Society's recent emphasis on action and its perceived neglect of spirituality; the financial crisis and the felt need to concentrate on our 'core purpose' - identified as spiritual nurture and outreach; and the mistrust of politics. There is also an individualistic view which believes that, while individuals have a responsibility to live out their individual faith, our corporate bodies have no such responsibility, or, if they have, no possibility of reaching the necessary unity. This last position will be considered when we come to look at the model of 'church' which we adopt, in the chapter entitled 'A "People of God"?'

Let us examine some of these assumptions which are tucked away in the positions of those who argue for 'the primacy of the spiritual'.

Changing Hearts or Systems

A long-standing strand of Quaker thinking asserts that you have to change people *before* systems. Part of a Meeting for Sufferings Minute from 1992 reads: 'We are a small church with the pretensions to change the world. But first we have to let God change us...'[16] This position is seldom closely argued but it persists in popular Quaker thinking. Why? It rightly stresses that unchanged hearts may undo any structural reform and that there is a dimension of moral and spiritual freedom in all social structures. But to move on to affirm that social change must wait for a change of heart is a timid middle class reaction which favours the status quo: if all structural problems could be dissolved into questions of personal transformation, society would never be ready to change. It takes but a moment's thought to see through the consequences of taking literally the injunction to change hearts first: South Africa would have had to wait until the hearts of the white ruling 'race' had been transformed; the Welfare State would have been postponed until either the politicians or the people or both were worthy enough; as for slavery, we would still be waiting to abolish it. We must root out this position wherever we see its seed germinating.

Rather let us unite with the 1925 Declaration: 'We must not think to wait until all are changed in heart, before beginning the task of setting up a social order more in accordance with the mind of Christ.'[17]

Being and Doing

I was once at a weekend at Glenthorne. In beautiful weather and surroundings we were sitting outside having our final Meeting for Worship. There was much ministry on the restorative nature of the weekend, which I was glad of; but it came to me that it needed to be put into a creative relationship with the harsh realities of life for many today. After my ministry, a thoughtful Friend was led to respond, also in ministry, that it was all right to let ourselves 'be' rather than 'do' for once.

How would you have reacted? I wrote her a long letter about how I saw the relationship of 'being' and 'doing'. As I wrote, I came to see clearly that, like 'faith' and 'action', it is a false opposition. Like all such pairs of words, it tends to suggest that one can only be *or* do, one *or* the other. This is, of course, nonsense. We are when we do. Sometimes, it is true, our action is mechanical, so routine that it does not feed our sense of creativity nor relate in a vital way to our deepest values. It could be said that we are not truly 'present' - to ourselves or others - at such times. But at other times what we do creates in us states of awareness that heighten our sense of being and are truly spiritual resources -

like compassion, or a steady sense of faithfulness, or solidarity with others.

As we 'are' when we 'do', so a state of 'being' is also a form of 'doing': all our more inward 'activities', like thinking, dreaming, reading and contemplating are also ways in which we are created or recreated in our relationship to ourselves, the world and God. They are preparations always; whatever we use our time in renders us more or less fit.

And, as with 'doing', these states of 'being' may be authentic or inauthentic, deep or superficial. Our inactivity may be sheer 'distractedness', may be as mechanical as our activity, or as untrue. Being present where we really are[18] is what counts; and true presence, in that sense, is a gift which knows no boundaries of 'being' or 'doing'. The spiritual dimension lies in the quality of each. And 'quality' here means attention, integrity and the transcendence of self. Those qualities are not easy to achieve, whether in reflection or in action but they apply to both. Unthinking use of a polarising opposition between 'being' and 'doing' obscures rather than reveals this truth.

I sense a danger here for contemporary Quakerism. To prioritise 'being' over 'doing' is to break apart the unity of faith-in-action/ action-in-faith. This leaning towards 'being' indicates perhaps the influence of the personal growth movement within contemporary Quakerism with its emphasis on nurturing one's self. The weariness of years of struggle against damaging social policies may also have created an understandable reaction. But the connection with a privatised spirituality, more at home with the search for personal serenity than with the struggle for justice, is clear. And yet, 'the inner life is not nurtured in order to hug to oneself some secret gain' in Elisabeth O'Connor's words.[19] 'Is not'? or 'should not be'?

Correcting the Society's Perceived Bias to Action

The opposition of 'being' (good) and 'doing' (bad) can be followed through in a number of different contexts. One of these is the increasing awareness in the 1970s that London Yearly Meeting's membership was rapidly changing, that few read the Bible, that spoken ministry was often cerebral, even tendentious; in short, that 'the spiritual' had been neglected in favour of political action, 'do-gooding', busyness.

Although awareness of the spiritual impoverishment of the Society came to a head in the 1970s the analysis was not new. In 1926 Neave Brayshaw refers to it as developing over the previous fifty years![20] Margaret Harvey encapsulated this worry in 1942: 'We belong to a spiritually shallow generation. In our Society this has been reflected in our concern over *causes*, our preoccupation with problems and in a noticeable absence of depth in spiritual experience and utterance.'[21] In neither case is there an explanation of the phenomenon. It seems likely that it had a lot to do with the progressive loss of the traditional religious language as liberal influences and secularisation became dominant.

This raises an intriguing question: were those most active in social responsibility less 'spiritual' than the less active? This can probably not be answered scientifically. But I offer my mother's life as a warning against easy assumptions. Her upbringing was rooted in the spirit of the 1895 Manchester Conference: liberal politically as well as theologically and fiercely rationalist. She threw herself into exhausting work for 'causes', for peace, for colonial freedom and for equality. She was active in the Labour Party. But she spoke very little about her faith - so far as I knew. One might have thought that she illustrated this theme of a shallow-rooted busyness. But how do we assess the faith of those who do not express themselves much in explicitly spiritual terms? When she died, suddenly in 1985, I found at her bedside her devotional reading. But, in any event, the selfless quality of her faithfulness was evidence enough of faith fullness.

Rufus Jones offers an alternative view of our humanitarian work to that offered by Neave Brayshaw and Margaret Harvey: 'There can be no question, I think, that our humanitarian work through the Service Committee has profoundly affected the attitude of the world, and particularly other churches towards us, but what is much more important is the fact that it has heightened our own spiritual power.'[22] That may well have held true for Britain too, at least in the inter war years.

However one judges these alternative analyses of the effects of our social witness, the renewed emphasis on our spiritual nurture in the last twenty years or so has been important for the life of the Yearly Meeting and has been the source of much good. It is my conviction, however, that it has had unintended negative side-effects: in particular, it has encouraged Friends to place 'spiritual nurture' in opposition to 'social witness', which is then increasingly envisaged as a purely human activity. Once it is seen as purely human, such activity, or suggestions for it, may be smothered with a groan. 'Busyness' itself has become a dirty word.

Busyness or the Culture of the Groan

I have heard Friends audibly groan when they hear that there is 'yet another' major issue to discuss. One wonders what the reaction would be if we had to gather for several days in Yearly Meeting in 1695 listening to extracts from George Keith's works, to weigh up the rights and wrongs of his treatment of and by his fellow Quakers! The culture of the groan is, in reality, an admission of an all-too-human sense of values. It suggests a state of mind that prioritises protection of the self, of personal comforts and routines; it may connect with the personal growth emphasis on self-fulfilment as a spiritual imperative. In either case there is suspicion of anything that smacks of the sacrificial. The thrust to nurture the spiritual life has paradoxically spawned this self-protective culture which, it seems to me, comes from the surface and not the spiritual depths.

I am not arguing that we should be proud of being busy. True faithfulness can certainly not be measured by the number of meetings we attend. (I once knew a member of a voluntary organisation who was constantly boasting about the number of evenings she was out and away from her husband.) Few of us entirely escape this treacherous sense of self-importance. Yet there is a true 'busyness' which is an openness to the moving of the spirit in a world whose soul and destiny are being struggled over. This true 'busyness' is spirit-filled, as in this description by Gordon Cosby of the mission work of the groups in the Church of the Saviour in Washington:

> We so carefully watch the limits of our health and strength, for some of us are very tired. We measure out the love that we give to others as from a medicine dropper. But under the baptism of the Spirit, I have seen limits disappear. People walk who can't walk - the too old, the too young, the too responsible, are all at it in the most irresponsible and refreshing way. I am deeply sympathetic with the limits - I understand them, but the power of the Spirit when the limits disappear is heady stuff.[23]

At the end of a long Monthly Meeting can we respond creatively to the the concerned Friend with a late message for us? The spiritual issue is not whether or not we are busy but whether our use of our time is in the hands of our self or the Godself within.

The Impact of the Financial Crisis

This reorientation towards spiritual renewal might have run its course. It might even have been subject to an opposite swing of the pendulum to allow Friends in Britain to face up to the enormity of the Conservative Government's assaults on our testimonies to equality and truth. Instead the financial crisis of the early 1990s broke, facing us with 'priorities'.

The language of priorities is analytical: it divides reality up into component parts - whereas the language of religion in general and of testimony in particular is the language of synthesis. The specific danger of the language of priorities is that it simplifies every issue into an 'either'/ 'or'.

The financial crisis created a discussion about what is essential and what is not. Maintaining the structure and nurturing local Meetings was essential. Enacted faith was less essential, even inessential. Some Friends envisaged the dismantling of QPS and QSRE almost in their entirety. Bob Needham, for example, wrote to *The Friend* in the following terms: 'QPS could focus down to the Quaker UN Offices, Quaker Council for European Affairs at Brussels, and the arms trade. The rest could be dumped. QSRE, homelessness, ditto.'[24] It is QHS which is 'our central central committee'. And he argues that it is so because it relates to *metanoia*, New Testament change in the individual.

I share his conviction that our faith has to be about our transformation. But what does such change mean unless the flame that has been lit provides warmth where there is need: 'The more purely the flame of contemplation burns, the more is it to be found in the end to inspire saving action'.[25] The United States of America is full of 'born again' Christians. They are, indeed, changed - often, alas, for the worse. Individual change which loses its connection to loving and just relationships is a travesty of the truly spiritual life. And a Quaker central structure which expressed Quaker faith by turning its back on the world would destroy Quaker spirituality.

Other priorities-led arguments are more damaging, because more apparently reasonable. For example, we are exhorted to do only what Quakers alone can do or 'what is uniquely our responsibility'. On the face of it this sounds sensible and hundreds of Friends have echoed it. But what does it really mean? Is there anything which only Quakers are involved in? Not the campaign against the arms trade. Not homelessness. Some aspects of our peacemaking perhaps?

It may be sensible to use most of our available resources where we can make a particularly needed impact; but this will not always be on our own. No other church would make such a claim. They recognise that they have a role in grappling with a range of issues, for their own education and to contribute to the embodiment of Christian values in the wider society. A contribution can be useful even when it is not unique. We badly need the humility to realise that we may be called to work in more humdrum ways than as pioneers.

A related position suggests that we should avoid overlapping with work others are doing. Again, it seems common sense. But what does it mean? Let us look at housing. There are a huge number of local and national organisations already at work. Our housing work connects with some of that, sometimes quite explicitly as with our role in helping Friends to join in the work of the Churches National Housing Coalition. But the core of our social witness work is in most cases helping Friends to face up to their spiritual responsibilities. No-one else can do that. All the time that priorities were being discussed and overlap was being warned against I never heard anyone give an example that could be acted upon. Was this just loose rhetoric serving a mood of retrenchment and losing touch with truth?

There is no doubt, however, that these themes touched a chord amongst Friends. They felt the need to concentrate on the 'essential' aspects of the work of the Society; and the essential was about spiritual nurture, implicitly opposed to witness - as though witness was not spiritual, nor nurture. In the words of a Meeting for Sufferings minute, which called for larger deductions to be made in corporate witness work than elsewhere: 'we affirm that it is our spiritual life which is the heart and essence of our living witness. We must keep our meetings'.[26] 'Spiritual life'? As opposed to what other sort of life that we have? Our spiritual life is the totality of our dedication to following God; our non-spiritual life is our inattention to the promptings of love and truth.

We can understand the implications of these arguments rather better if we take a close look at some of the metaphors which are associated with them.

The Roots and the Fruit

This traditional biblical metaphor has been frequently used to suggest that the spiritual roots must grow strong - first. This is a very important claim. It seems to be common sense. It justifies the commonplace of Quaker discourse that we need to put ourselves to rights spiritually before we do anything else. (See pp 24-25) It is clearly related to the notion of 'the primacy of the spiritual'.

In fact, this metaphor turns out to be very problematical. If 'spiritual life' contains the meaning which was given to it at the outset - our relationship to God through the totality of our relationship with the rest of the world - we cannot get our spiritual life right *before* the rest. Any attempt to do this separates out 'the spiritual' from the rest, as though 'the spiritual' was a distinct area of life rather than an understanding of life in its ultimate significance.

The other problem is that the organic metaphor is taken too literally. Of course roots do produce plants which produce fruits. However, it is the fruits which are the seeds which first create the roots. The metaphor is cyclical, not static. And that is our spiritual experience: we may grow through study or prayer, or by committed action or enforced changes of lifestyle or relationship. What really transforms us does not always result from study groups or contemplative retreats. If the emphasis on spiritual development is too 'study bound' we could find that not only is our service weakened by being downgraded in our priorities but that our spiritual life may shrivel for lack of substance. It may remain academic, poetic or bucolic and out of touch. Any static understanding of this metaphor is actually subversive of the testimony to the sacramental nature of the whole of life.

Recharging the Batteries

But the most commonplace metaphor sees in Meeting for Worship the function of recharging one's spiritual batteries. The unspoken assumption is that, in Meeting for Worship, we are plugged into God in a special way: God is taken in for an hour. The rest of the week, that God-given energy is inexorably drained away. I recognise that Meeting for Worship is one of the places where our energy is sustained; and I can understand the experience of exhausted welfare professionals and others. Nonetheless the metaphor is dangerous, both for what it reveals of a self-preoccupied and therapeutic motivation for attending Meeting for Worship and because it reverses our understanding of our access to God at all times.

The truth is that we gain spiritual energy in all sorts of circumstances, sometimes the most exhausting and demanding of them. Take Doris Lessing's *The Diaries of Jane Somers*.[27] The narrator is transformed - spiritually we would say - by her experience of caring for an elderly neighbour. As the blurb puts it:

> Smart, well off and successful editor of a glossy magazine, Janna Somers is in control of her destiny. But the death of her first husband and then of her mother opens a space in Janna's fashionable armour that she hadn't expected. And into that space creeps Maudie Fowler, a stubborn old woman both frail and alone. As the difficult friendship between them grows, Janna's vision of the world and of herself begins to deepen and change.

In short, what breaks open Janna's glossy persona is her often costly friendship with Maudie. It transforms her.

Janna's batteries are charged as she is changed by difficult and wearing action in the world. This is much better Quakerism than the usual version of this metaphor in our Meetings, which implicitly assumes that faith is revitalised in Meeting for Worship and exhausted in action in the secular world. Do we really live on that sort of basis? Do we have no experience of 'love' growing 'stronger when you give it away'? That in giving we receive? Isn't that the extraordinary divine economy, unlike the monetary economy where we receive the wage and the money disappears progressively?

If we can be with God during the washing up, on a car journey, canvassing on the doorstep, on a soup run or lobbying an M.P. then we are not only regenerated during Meeting for Worship or other quiet times. This metaphor makes Meeting for Worship too different from the rest of our life and is implicitly dualistic. It is out of harmony with our belief in the sacramental nature of the whole of life. It may only be a metaphor - probably the dominant contemporary metaphor of the action of Meeting for Worship - but its implications undermine some of the foundations of Quaker faith.

The Spiritual and the Political

Contemporary Quakerism offers few full-blooded examples of the dualism between the spiritual and the temporal. However, the related opposition of the spiritual and the political is easier to detect. It takes a number of forms. Sometimes we are told that Friends should not corporately take up political positions; or that this should only be done when there is unanimity. Sometimes there is a sharper opposition between politics and religion in general. Often this opposition is found in individual Friends' responses to corporate Quaker statements. The Yearly Meeting Statement on Poverty is a case in point.[28] A number of Friends were deeply shocked by it and met on several occasions to consider how to respond.

The opening paragraph of Janette Denley's letter to *The Friend* gives the flavour:

The statement on Poverty issued from Friends House and published in the press on June 10 is unfeeling and deeply hurtful to the many Members of the Society who have a concern for their fellow men [*sic*] but whose sympathies do not lie with a left-wing political group.[29]

In the same issue Bertrand Roberson also 'finds it difficult not to take it as a party political exhortation'.

That Statement is now in *Quaker Faith and Practice*. And everything that London Yearly Meeting said in it in 1987 seems to have been confirmed since as the signs of the times have become more and more glaring. Of course the Statement was - rightly - political; as was its context. Its impact will not have been neutral. None of which matters if we are clear that our corporate Quaker political interventions are spirit-based. The Poverty Statement came from an overwhelming conviction that we could not be true to our testimony to equality without expressing solidarity with those who were suffering the worst effects of inequality. The Testimonies should play a crucial role in ensuring that any political actions are rooted in faith. I return to these questions in a later chapter.

I have examined a series of interpretations of the relationship between faith and action. I have tried to show how some of these positions are mistaken or un-Quakerly. Cumulatively I believe that they represent a weakening experience of the inseparable links between faith and action. Shortly I shall suggest how we might repair this structural damage. But first I need to show how my experience has led me to these words.

My Experience of Faith and Action

These words are not just intellectual positions which I have adopted out of pure reason. They are the fruits of my experience. I know that faith can be deepened - even reformed - in action. I know that in 'doing' I have experienced states of 'being' that cannot be discovered otherwise.

In all my spiritual journey so far the most powerful experience of a new quality of light breaking through came about when I agreed to stand as a local candidate for the Labour Party in what was then a Conservative stronghold in North-East Fife. Previously my political activity had drawn on reserves of stubborn faithfulness just to keep attending meetings; but nothing happened to me - and very little impact was made on anyone else! My engagement was too limited to open me up. However, campaigning had been nurtured into me and I threw myself into election campaigns year after year with tremendous intensity and utterly foolish zeal - since the cause was well- nigh hopeless and what I could achieve for the people of the area was minimal.

But I began to open my ears and eventually my heart to what the people in the old radical paper mill village of Guardbridge wanted to share with me: their sense of loss of political faith, their conviction that no-one cared about them, their cynicism and confusion. As I did so - several times for an hour or more on the doorstep or in people's homes - it was my heart that was opened up by the openness and pain of those who spoke with me. My heart went out to them with a flowing intensity which I had never experienced before. And the experience lasted beyond the particular occasion in an almost physical sense of being 'drawn out towards'. And then it became a way into prayer, which had been very difficult for me, without an orthodox sense of a personal God.

Eventually, I was led to change my job and home and to work, and later, to live, amongst people like those in Guardbridge who had given me something immensely precious. That took time, while my 'creaturely' self wanted to hang on to many tangible and intangible things. As the transformation worked its way in me, reading and Meeting for Worship also played their part. St Andrews Meeting was a small, lively meeting; we came to Meeting for Worship and to Preparative and Monthly Meetings to try to discern the things that really mattered. It was as though something transforming might happen at any time in the fellowship of the Meeting and in Meeting for Worship itself.

For me, the decisive shoves occurred when its Midweek Meeting studied Woolman, whom I had not read before. Here was a life which demonstrated an inspiring consistency of word and deed. The challenge of that reading shadowed me in Meeting for Worship. I was led to minister in ways that called me to a position that I had not yet reached, and then demanded a greater consistency between the words uttered and the life lived. However that ministry spoke to others, it certainly played its part in changing me. The final nail was driven home by Sewell Harris' ministry at Yearly Meeting in Warwick in 1982 in which he quoted from John Drinkwater's poem, *A Prayer*, the final stanza of which reads:

> Knowledge we ask not - knowledge thou hast lent,
> But, Lord, the will - there lies our bitter need,
> Give us to build above the deep intent
>   The deed, the deed.

I need to add: these things are only written by way of breathing life into the themes I am exploring; the changes were small and I know all-too-well how far apart my words and deeds still are. What matters here is to show that spiritual growth is part of real living not a project apart. It often requires some major new event in our lives to open ourselves up. Study is important, but it is not enough. The spiritual is vital and, in a sense, it is primary not because it comes first but because it is what makes sense of life in all its aspects.

Conclusion

What challenges and opportunities for the Society of Friends in Britain can be imagined from this analysis? We have changed less of late than most denominations in our understanding of faith in action; indeed we have not changed much since the 1920s. Such as we are, what can we affirm now? And how can we be led beyond the place we have reached?

Firstly, we should celebrate corporately our deep conviction that there is no part of life where the spiritual is out of bounds. No separation of the spiritual and the social. We could endorse both Wilfred Allott's 'The social problem is a spiritual problem'[30] and Horace Pointing's 'a truly religious life cannot be lived without a sense of social responsibility'.[31] As a community we would affirm our experience that the spiritual is not restricted to special subjects or special places. Ultimately our ideal is to fuse the whole of our life by the spirit of prayer, so that we experience it simultaneously in its present moment and through the illumination of the eternal: 'What is sought is not alternation [of the inner and the outer] but simultaneity, worship undergirding every moment.'[32]

Secondly we should be firm and clear in our understanding that spiritual growth necessarily entails consequences for our action in the world. If spiritual growth is about making our relation to God closer, and if love of God is inseparable from love of our neighbours in the widest sense, then to grow spiritually will be to grow closer to their life and readier to act in their interests.

Thirdly, we need to learn that action is not a mere consequence of spiritual growth. It may be a means to it. The process of breaking through to new levels of awareness is not always the result of pure thought.It often comes from concrete engagement. Hence Baron von Hugel's advice to Evelyn Underhill was 'more than anything else he could suggest, to throw out the cerebral accent in her religion and to break open her heart to the needs of all, she should devote two evenings a week to "visiting the poor"'.[33] We might not use quite the same form of social action if we gave that advice; more crucial is whether it would occur to us to give such advice at all. Do we recognise that we may need our hearts broken open if God is to break through?

Sometimes, indeed, a half awareness can be brought to full realisation by acting it out. As Friends we place great emphasis on truthfulness and on being clear. Do we sometimes look and wait for clearness so long that we never make the leap? John

Harvey shows us a messier picture of the connection of faith and action: 'Not "Bring your belief to the proof of action, testify to it by practising it" but "Bring your half belief into the powerhouse of co-action that it may become full belief"'.[34] Our beliefs may need testing out in practice before they are confirmed.

A fourth position that we can strongly reaffirm is that charity is not enough. The Christian tradition of individual almsgiving and our Quaker inheritance of Victorian philanthropy are inadequate expressions of Christian love at any time, and all the more so when the development of democracy has given us responsibility for the well-being of our fellow citizens as a whole. That means that we fully acknowledge that our responsibility extends to remedying the causes of social evils.

Our tradition in this respect is neither as long nor as honourable as we sometimes think, but we did take significant strides forward at the end of the nineteenth and beginning of the twentieth centuries. Lucy Fryer Morland, in her Swarthmore Lecture in 1918 traces the gradual recognition that social responsibility entails 'dealing with the framework of society'. She does so, in part, by examining successive editions of the General Advices. In 1834 these limited their social range to 'liberality to the poor', 'integrity in business' and 'special care for servants'. The 1861 version was very strong on the virtue of self-help. It was only in 1911 that the new stress on the causes of social evils came in:

> Do you, as disciples of the Lord Jesus, take a living interest in the social conditions of those around you? [...] Do you seek to understand the causes of social evils and to take your right share in the endeavour to remove them?'[35]

Thereafter this theme runs like a thread through the 1920s and 30s. For example, the Committee on War and the Social Order reported to Yearly Meeting in 1921 on the urgent need for a new social order and that Quaker money 'can be more usefully employed in helping to bring about the changes necessary than by palliating individual cases of hardship, though the latter often seem the more obvious and pressing.'[36] We cannot restrict Christian love to immediate succour.

Our stress on fundamental change to the structures which create individual suffering is strong. We have a great many members involved in single issue pressure groups and in political parties - perhaps a higher proportion than in other denominations. The exceptional support Friends have shown for the relatively new Parliamentary Liaison work is another indication: probably no other area of Friends' central work has been more strongly defended against cuts during the last years. We have much to be glad of.

Yet here lies our challenge and our opportunity. Consider, for example, our housing work. How much of the huge amount of effort over the last ten years has been devoted to changing government policy? As opposed to serving on management committees of housing associations or Quaker homes for the elderly or serving soup at an open Christmas and the like? Nearer 10% or 75%? No-one knows, but I guess it is less than 10% and probably less than 5%. Why is this so?

One reason is because conventional political campaigning can lack much sense of engagement both with the people who exercise power, and with those who are suffering the consequences. Hence the difficulty in sustaining the work of the Churches National Housing Coalition in its unique attempt to create local ecumenical pressure groups to work for improvements in housing policy. It is hard graft for uncertain and long-term results. It requires unfashionable amounts of dogged determination.

A second reason, some argue, is that political action is a special gift which not all Friends possess. Once more, this seems eminently reasonable. A simple matter of gifts and ministries. Nonetheless it is worth reflecting on. Would anyone argue that some Friends should be exempted from expressing their spirituality in neighbourliness, peacefulness, or forgiveness, because these involved special gifts? It cannot be that some of us are exempted from embodying our faith in our lives. However, only a few of us are supposed to have the special gift of involvement with the structural issues of policies and politics. That is held to be an optional extra.

Understandable though this reaction is, it is not good enough. Historically it has been difficult for most people to take responsibility for the policies of their country. Power has usually been exercised by tiny, often hereditary, minorities. So, when the world's major religions were developing, democracy was absent. However, that responsibility is now part of our day-to-day lives. It needs to become integral to our spirituality. Knowledge is needed, certainly; but concerned people are equally important and that is not a special gift. With some assistance most people could play their part in bringing their faith to bear on political life. Perhaps the churches - and Britain Yearly Meeting with them - need to see it as a spiritual challenge to encourage the preparation of their members for this service.

A third reason for our inability to fulfil our promise to attend to the structures is that we are uncomfortable with the political. It is true that Yearly Meeting has minuted several times its recognition that Friends must act politically. But, often when the issue arises in concrete practice, Friends base their reaction on their prudential fear of disunity as much as on their sense of divine leading.

This may be the sharpest challenge we face. Do we withdraw from action on the social order, because we mistrust the central structure that could sustain such a process, or because we have lost confidence that we can corporately be led into unity on such large matters, which, from the world's standpoint, seem too divisive? Do we carry on as we are with a relatively low key political contribution? Or do we develop our tradition of corporate concern to work on the causes of social evils?

Our starting point is to reaffirm and celebrate our inheritance of the testimony to the sacramental nature of the whole of life. Our challenge is to work out its meaning in practice. This would mean a much more consistent, corporate effort to express the implications of our faith values for social policy. Yes! In the hurly burly of the run-up to an election as much as at any other time. Of course we run risks in any move in this direction; it would be a bumpier ride. It would involve sharp disagreements at times. But Friends had their disagreements in the past. Sweet reasonableness is not synonymous with truth - or discipleship. The development of such a position would be to work on our strengths.

We would do it if we could all say with Daniel Berrigan:

> The time will shortly be upon us, if it is not already here, when the pursuit of contemplation becomes a strictly subversive activity ... I am convinced that contemplation, including the common worship of the believing, is a political act of the highest value, implying the riskiest of consequences to those taking part.[37]

We will do it when we see, really see, that the values of the world are destroying the values on which our faith is based.

- Chapter 2 -
Context: THE CULTURAL CLIMATE

Once we have dismantled a world in which larger
virtues held sway, what is left are success and self-
expression, the key values of an individualistic culture.

Jonathan Sacks[1]

Historical Introduction

For more than three hundred years in Western Europe we have
been living in a culture which has pushed God out of one area of
life after another; so much so that several times God has been
declared dead. This process was, in very important ways, a
liberation of reason, science and individual creativity from the
shackles of superstition and absolutism. But it also led directly
to a cultural climate in which truth has been shattered into relative
fragments; in which no expression of ultimate purpose has proved
resistant to the corrosive force of nihilism.

This human adventure replaced the all-embracing absolutism
of the Catholic world-view with a more fragmentary, subjective
view of truth: it replaced the authority of religion by reason; it
subverted traditional wisdom by science and the individual's
unfettered right to question. In the process all the old absolutes
were undermined. Philosophically, these included truth and
beauty and justice; socially they included the organised church,
the institutions of justice and the ruling elite. It overthrew the
divinely appointed social order replacing it with representative
government and later democracy. Its political philosophy was
liberalism and its economic order capitalist. And its tendency
was always towards secularising human understanding. Its end
point is the autonomous individual as sole judge of right and
wrong in a world devoid of transcendence and of meaning.

Amongst the many revolutions which drove these
developments forward were the Enlightenment, the French

Revolution, Romanticism and the Industrial Revolution. Later both anthropological and psychological research added to the sense that values were relative to time and circumstance and had no objective validity: "the astonishing diversity of behaviour patterns ... instils serious doubts as to the claim of any single moral code to more than purely local and relative validity. Indeed the notion that certain judgements of what is good and bad in conduct are *true* falls into discredit."[2]

When events gathered speed as they did during the French Revolution the shock to orthodox Christianity was utterly disorientating. A French Catholic, Félicité de Lamennais, expressed his bewilderment at the disintegration of the Catholic world order, which had so long guaranteed human meaning by assigning everything a role in the overarching providential plan. This is what he wrote:

> It is in vain that we summon to our aid human reason, for it is a fragile defence against doubt! or rather it is a river in spate which breaks down every bank, sweeps away and drowns every certainty when it arrives and flows over what we know and understand. Every century, every country, every man has their individual opinions: they are as variable as dreams and often in contradiction one with another. You see them, like faint meteors shining for a moment before being swallowed up in eternal night.[3]

It is not surprising that such developments were a less profound shock to Quakerism than to Catholicism. Firstly Friends' belief in the individual's direct communication with God and their suspicion of doctrinal or credal positions meant that they were less threatened by rationalism and science. Secondly they had created a particular fusion of theocratic and democratic elements in their own self-government, which predisposed them to accept democratic reforms. Thirdly, from the earliest days, they were prime movers in the capitalist revolution with all its implications for the growth of individualism[4] and secularism.

Notwithstanding this basis for an accommodation with the developing 'open society', Friends were protected from its most far-reaching implications by their emphasis on their own closed tradition. Secularisation and individualism were held at bay for a time. That protection was swept away around the middle of the nineteenth century when disownment for marrying out was done away with. Even then the evangelicals' theological orthodoxy remained a final 'hedge' against the rational, critical spirit. That hedge was uprooted by, amongst others, the authors of *A Reasonable Faith* and the leading lights of the 1895 Manchester Conference. Once the modern period of Liberal Quakerism had become established Friends no longer had the shelter of any hedge against the prevailing winds of moral relativism and sweeping secularisation.

The Manchester Conference is the well-known turning point towards a much fuller accommodation with the modern world. Thereafter the voice of London Yearly Meeting falls broadly within the liberal spectrum of spiritual beliefs. A powerful commitment to human reason, a belief in progress, a spirit of open-ended enquiry and of toleration were all characteristic. These features were, in turn, to lead to the more relativistic, secular and individualist spirit of Britain Yearly Meeting in the late twentieth century.[5]

What kept nihilism at bay up to at least 1940 was another powerful ideology, the belief in progress. Friends' thinking at that time is dominated by it. Hardly a Swarthmore Lecture is given where this note is not struck. The mood is optimistic partly because huge strides have been made towards equality through the development of education and democratic rights, partly also because the severe crisis of capitalism suggested that exploitation and injustice might soon be more radically overcome.

That is how I remember the spirit of my Quaker upbringing in the 1940s and 50s. Even in the harsh climate of the Cold War - which did distance Friends from an earlier optimism - and even after the illustration of the reality of human evil in the holocaust and the atomic bomb, the values of the spirit still seemed to be increasingly embodied in the real world: colonised peoples would win their freedom and, in Britain, in the new Welfare State, everyone could look forward to a decent job and a reasonable standard of living.

Up to the 1950's there was, therefore, little reason to question the new Quaker liberal consensus. Even now the question for us is not whether the Enlightenment was or was not a good thing, nor whether the 1895 Conference was or was not a right turning point for the Society of Friends in Great Britain. Both those liberations were essential. The question is rather: have those trends now gone too far? Have we followed them under clear guidance as to their rightness or have we simply followed the times rather than the signs of the times? In 1895 London Yearly Meeting gave impetus to the new direction in which it was being led. It is time to pause and consider whether we have travelled too far along that path.

Relativism and Nihilism

> Relativism deprives us of the means - indeed of the right
> - to express deep revulsion.

Ernest Gellner[6]

Let me begin by telling you the journey I went through, as I think it may be representative. It is the story of the loss of confidence in a transcendent basis for a Quaker way of life through the impact of a relativistic culture of the purely human. And then, of its rediscovery.

I was a birthright Friend. I had been actively involved in the Society through my local Meeting in Swansea, Sidcot Summer School, Junior Yearly Meeting etc. After leaving school I studied French at University. My special subject was 'The Modern French Novel', which, at that time, was Malraux, St Exupery, Camus and

Sartre. These were writers who had grappled with the crisis of absolute values. They had rejected them, and, with them, all notions of God. I remember the powerful attraction of this tradition, with Nietzsche as its godfather and the dramatists of the absurd, Beckett, Ionesco and others as its progeny. The great theme of this literature was the relativisation of Truth: if there was no absolute, there was no Truth. The glass was shattered into fragments; each individual, as Lamennais so feared, had but a fragment of truth; it was impossible to judge between them. I became more or less agnostic without cutting myself off from the Society.

I became a lecturer in French and taught these authors. Slowly, as I taught them, I became aware that, if they exposed the impossibility of proving absolute Truth, their nihilism created just as many problems as it apparently solved. Camus, like Malraux, for all his nihilistic theories, had little difficulty in deciding to join the Resistance against the occupying German Nazi forces in France. But, if there is no Truth and nothing has greater value than anything else, why risk death? If all is subjective, who is to say that Nazism is any worse than any other ideology? How, even, can torture be condemned? In a very telling admission in his *Letters to a German Friend*, he writes:

> For a long time we both believed that the world was devoid of ultimate purpose ... Today I tell myself that if I had really followed you in your beliefs I would have to approve of what you have done. ... In truth I, who thought I believed as you do, I could not find any reason to oppose you save a passionate taste for justice which, in the final analysis, seemed to me just as far removed from the process of reasoning as a love affair out of the blue.[7]

So, once nihilism has destroyed certainty it is itself undermined by doubt. That was the movement in Malraux and Camus and Sartre. This was also my experience in the 1960s. Over a long period of time a conviction strengthened in me that the death of God and of the absolute was less sure than had been supposed. In God's absence, death might seem logically final, yet somehow love transcended it. Truth might be difficult to define, or grasp, but a belief in the absence of ultimate Truth involved a tissue of contradictions and was almost impossible to live by. Besides, my experience increasingly found the ultimate in moments of love, forgiveness and transparency. I knew that I did not live as though moral values were purely relative; and I knew that I could not live as though signposts were like weather vanes, pointing successively towards each and every point of the compass.

It was the same process with aesthetic values. While teaching, I was struck time and again by how helpless students felt, caught as they were between the demand to acknowledge critical standards and their feeling that it was all sheer opinion. We face the same alternative as in morality: it is impossible to prove aesthetic value, yet it is absurd to deny it.

Aesthetically, the argument runs like this: it is impossible to prove the superiority of, say, Shakespeare to a Mills and Boon novelette; if someone asserts that the Mills and Boon is better it is just her/his word against mine; full stop. I know, from discussions with my students, that the argument is felt to be very convincing; but I believe it to be mistaken. We may not be able to know whether Homer or Dante is the greater writer; we may get some value judgements wrong and have to revise them. That does not mean that value judgements are impossible.

Shakespeare is greater than a Mills and Boon novelette. If that were not so we would expect as many of his fans to be converted to Mills and Boon as vice versa. That is unlikely; almost no one who has appreciated the richness of Shakespeare will gravitate to the Mills and Boon; development is the other way.

Many Friends experience this confusion. They assume that if there is no easily demonstrated formulation, and no objective knowledge of universal Truth, then there is no Truth, only subjective opinion. Of course they do not live their lives on that basis; nonetheless it corrodes their spiritual energy and weakens all corporate forms of it. Even if we cannot capture Truth in a glass jar, it is our job to celebrate our glimpses of it. There is no need to be defeatist or defensive, or even apologetic about those things which speak to us of ultimate value. Including God.

It is because I have been through this evolution that I am convinced that many Friends have given in far too easily to the sceptical, relativist and individualist implications of much contemporary culture. Should we now be labelled children of the Enlightenment rather than Children of the Light? I am not suggesting that the Enlightenment should be scorned; we are rightly influenced by it in many ways. Where it has questioned arbitrary absolutism, both religious and political, where it has insisted on the role of human reason, where it has fostered tolerance and the 'principled relativism' of respect for other cultures[8], where it has celebrated the individual as the locus of the search for truth - in all these we have reason to be grateful.

But, particularly since the Second World War, we have travelled ever further in those directions. We have now gone too far towards an all-too-easy-going relativism. You only have to hear the lazy Quaker commonplace that there are as many Quaker views on anything as there are Quakers, to understand my point. All too easily this means that there is no way of choosing between them; every belief is equally valid. It is a condition which has been termed 'terminal tolerance'.[9]

Timothy Gorringe sees this moral relativism as the counterpart intellectually to the material effects of international capitalism. Just as the whole world has become our supermarket for material goods, so there is a supermarket of ideas from which we can pick and choose:

> Philosophies, religions, ethical theories are there along with perfumes, foodstuffs and curtaining, to be chosen from and consumed as we will, a smorgasbord in which there are no absolute preferences.[10]

I am reminded of John Punshon's memorable and profoundly disturbing metaphor for our Society, 'supermarket Quakerism'. He regrets that Friends choose their spiritual beliefs as they choose their shopping in a supermarket: 'One may wander round the Friendly emporium selecting from the shelves, whatever nourishment one chooses, with very little restriction.'10

The dominance of this relativistic morality and metaphysics amongst contemporary British Friends is gravely damaging to many aspects of Quakerism. In particular it weakens the basis for corporate action both because it spreads the assumption that agreement will be impossible and because it undermines our business method which is based on a common search for the will of God for the group. Its individualism provides poor defences against the secular world; it destroys the sense that our faith seeks to implement timeless values in a world of change.

This new Quaker approach has been picked up from the surrounding culture. As we have seen, there were good reasons to take on board a questioning of the old absolutes. We need now to question the questioning. As with Malraux and Camus, Quaker relativism leads up a blind alley: we know it is not true, because those who profess it do not really believe it. Faced with evil they will reject that evil not because they do not like it but because it is fundamentally wrong. Timothy Gorringe sums it up: 'This kind of relativism expresses not a generous tolerance but a weary or cynical giving up on truth.'[12]

Thus, for many Friends now, there is no ultimate reference point. If our faith, our morality, our political values, have no objective basis, then, with our death, they will sink into oblivion. The meaningfulness of our lives depends on their connection with a transcendence, something ultimate which endures. A purely immanent inner light which was limited to our cultural and historical particularity would die with each of our deaths. Without a transcendent dimension, relativism spreads everywhere; it is a quagmire within which we are sucked into the anti-spiritual terrain of the absurd.

Secularisation

> The Church is no longer the central focus of life. One of
> its functions after another has been taken from it and
> left it stripped like an autumn tree.
>
> Rufus Jones[13]

The despiritualisation of the world is a dominant trend which
has already been sketched in. I have shown how it squeezes
religion out of most areas of life, leaving it on the margins as a
special activity for a minority. Religious language is little
encountered in business, politics and leisure - except as metaphor;
it has only a marginal place in most educational and media
contexts. It still accompanies the key stages of life - birth, marriage
and death - but as a tradition without great vitality. In much
ordinary conversation it is totally absent.

In such conditions secular assumptions will colonise us if we
offer little resistance to them. If that happens our spirituality
will be confined to the special 'reservations' that are left. Early
Friends had the defence of the doctrine of the two worlds - being
in the world but not *of* it - which we have discarded for a much
more monist world view. Have we lost something which could
help us resist?

We need to remember that Friends until recently have tried to
protect themselves from the 'world'. At first they made a clear
distinction between living as renewed by the spirit and living in
the world's way. Later, they kept themselves visibly separate from
the world by dress, language and the like. We have seen that this
status as a 'peculiar people' was discarded in the mid nineteenth
century. Most commentators see that change as positive: it seemed
to bring to a close the period when Friends were stuck in a
backwater, culturally impoverished, intellectually stagnating, and
declining in numbers.

Since 1850 the Society has moved steadily towards an
accommodation with contemporary culture. Quaker spirituality

is increasingly stamped with the experimental and rationalist temper of the times. Quakerism becomes a form of 'natural religion' - spiritual experience is inherent in human nature rather than dependent on divine revelation. An increasing stress on the inner light as a natural inborn faculty also blurred the former opposition between world and spirit.

At the same time as Friends moved closer to the dominant intellectual framework of the age, they also identified increasingly clearly with the democratic system and its associated aspiration towards social progress and greater equality. They felt that democracy and ethical socialism were steps on the way to the Kingdom of God. Since no fundamental conflict existed between world and spirit Friends could identify with the former, in its trajectory at least, if not entirely with its existing state. This relationship continued to exercise a powerful attraction to Friends into the post Second World War world of full employment and the Welfare State. Despite all the differences over peace, over the pace of decolonisation, etc., the aspirations of Friends and the direction of social development were in harmony.

What happens, however, when faith and world point in opposite directions? What is the price of accommodation then? We have to choose: either we acquiesce, more or less uneasily in the dominant cultural values or we emerge from the relative comfort of accommodation into the harsher world of dissent.

And the conditions which led to a greater identification of faith and world have changed fundamentally. In the last twenty years or so society has become vastly more unequal; consumerism has developed far beyond the meeting of basic needs; the worship of money has become more unbridled; the self-centred individual has become a role model. The times have changed and few of us see social and political change as working towards the Kingdom. The values of world and spirit have moved apart.

Why have we been so slow to adapt to these changed conditions? Firstly, if the Enlightenment was the moment when the transcendental and the absolute were tamed by the human and the relative, then contemporary Quakerism is certainly its heir; with our largely immanent faith in that of God within we have little sense of another dimension, little sense of a world beyond our own. The black and white world of prophecy and of early Friends has dissolved into shades of grey in our time.

Secondly the Society, in its increasing identification with the world has implicitly accepted the long-standing process of secularisation. We are immersed in a world of secular interpretations of almost everything. Many assume that this world, in its materiality, is all that there is. According to Caroline Graveson, 'a larger proportion of our time is spent in secular occupation than ever before'.[14] The phrase 'secular occupation' tells a tale. If all life is sacramental, even secular occupation is only secular if we approach it in that way.

What is certainly true is that Friends today spend a far higher proportion of their time in contexts which are secular - work, voluntary organisations, leisure, the media. In the past much more time was spent in Quaker contexts, whether on Quaker business or simply with an extended Quaker family and Quaker friends. What is important in this is the transmission of values. Friends today spend a much greater part of their time absorbing the values conveyed by the secular media and the forces of capitalist consumerism than was previously the case. Early Friends by contrast absorbed the values of their Quaker community rather than of the world at large.

A letter to *The Friend* aptly illustrates this. The writer asked that it should appear less frequently as some Friends could not cope with so much information every week. Do such Friends read a daily newspaper or watch half an hour of television a day? It takes between one and two hours a week to read *The Friend* from cover to cover. What percentage of the words we read or hear will come from a Quaker, or even a spiritual perspective? This strikes me as an extraordinarily revealing example of a prevailing Quaker belief that we can be Quakers in a secular world effortlessly. It seems that we are not only wary of indoctrinating others but ourselves. We are in danger of becoming - to coin a word - 'undoctrinated' Friends.

But how can we maintain in our daily lives a sense of the ongoing baptism by the spirit, instead of letting the tide of secularised materialist values immerse us? The public world of commercial transactions, of advertising and the rest measures everything on the scale of self-interest. It is true that Friends, by and large, have not 'bought into' this ideology as readily as into the cultural processes which have accompanied it. Nevertheless we have not found a way of creating a consistent stance, still less a practice, of opposition to it. We seem not to have fully woken up to the enormous power of the materialist ideology which is exerted over us.

Elisabeth O'Connor shows how easy it is to be infiltrated by secular values: 'We', she writes, 'who would be shaped by Christ are shaped by headlines and the counsel of friends who do not know Him.'[15] I recognise the diagnosis. You can save tax by fictitiously charging your wife or husband for cleaning the room you use at home for an office; your bike is stolen when it was not locked securely and you invent a story to cover your mistake; you charge personal expenses to your business account; you are happy to get that repair done cheaper by paying cash-in-hand, knowing full well that it will escape the tax net. Everyone does it. These small daily decisions are in some ways the hardest tests because it is so easy for them to appear to be outside the scope of our spirituality. It is easier to follow unthinkingly the conventional wisdom of the secularised world.

The question that I shall turn to in Chapter Five is this: how can we ensure that both major decisions - jobs, housing, money and time - and the small-scale choices in everyday life - shopping, travelling, holidays - are all consciously, and then naturally and simply, part of our practice of faith?

But first we need to examine a number of other changes in contemporary Quakerism which seem to me to stem from the prevailing secular climate of ideas. These are firstly the abandonment of the doctrine of the two worlds and the related weakening of the testimony to the sacramental nature of the whole of life; secondly, the introduction of the 'personal growth' approach into Quakerism and the related rejection of sacrifice, sin and guilt.

The Two Worlds

Fundamental to the Christian spiritual tradition is the opposition of world and spirit. This has taken many forms. Sometimes it contrasts the essential unreality of our earthly existence with life after death. That version of the dualism, which devalues our life on earth, has not been attractive to Friends. The position of early Friends was quite different. The contrast which they returned to time and again was that between living in the Spirit here and now as opposed to living in the world on the world's terms. This is how Isaac Penington puts it:

> Now our work in the world is ... to live like God; not to own anything in the world which God does not own; to forget our country, our kindred, our father's house, and to live like persons of another country, of another kindred, of another family; not to do anything of ourselves, and which is pleasing to the old nature."[16]

We can appreciate in this quotation the very sharp nature of the opposition of the two worlds. There is absolutely no spirit of accommodation to the age. A war is to be waged, a spiritual war, the Lamb's War against the spirit of the world.

This approach of early Friends has been extensively criticised. It can seem to limit God's work and presence in and through the ordinary everyday human world too much. At all events the two worlds approach has largely disappeared from British Quakerism. I believe we are the poorer for its loss. The polarisation may have been too sharp. On the other hand our modern Quaker stress on the world, not as the antagonist of the spirit, but simply as the context in which it appears is far too one-dimensional.

The Sacramental Nature of the Whole of Life

This testimony is fundamental to Quakerism. It implies that there can be no separation into distinct spiritual and secular spheres. We have been justly committed to that and have used it against the false dualism of 'pie in the sky' Christianity, where existence in this world is simply to be endured pending our translation to heaven.

However, this testimony is not necessarily opposed to all dualism, such as the dualism implied by the doctrine of the two worlds. To affirm that the whole of life is sacramental does not mean that God is equally manifest in every aspect of life.

I suspect that our view of the sacramental nature of all life was distorted as Quakerism came under increasing secular pressure. Gradually, it lost sight of its origin in the opposition between life lived in God's presence and life lived on the secular assumptions of 'the world'. Increasingly it was distorted into a vague pantheistic sense that love is everywhere and that humankind is fundamentally good. But, as E.B. Castle pointed out:

> There is a great difference between believing that man is fundamentally good and believing that there is something fundamentally good in man.[17]

I would go further. The testimony to the sacramental nature of the whole of life positively requires the dualism of the two worlds. Why? It is very simple, though I have heard Friends tie themselves in knots over it: the testimony does not suggest that everything that is thought, said and done witnesses positively to God's nature; what it implies is that there is no situation where there is nothing of God to be said. When we lie and grab and hate and the rest we are denying the nature of God; we are living against God. Of course, our situation is potentially redeemable and the possibility of responding to God remains in us. But we are not expressing God in our lying and grabbing and hatred. The testimony is based on the conviction that there is no part of life which is irrelevant to the struggle between that which is of God and that which is not.

Personal Growth - or Sacrifice, Sin and Guilt

Since the First World War the accommodation of Quakerism with liberalism, rationalism and democracy has had the effect of rendering suspect a whole range of religious experience which was essential to early Friends. Almost all talk of sacrifice, discipline and will and of evil, sin and guilt has vanished. They have been supplanted in Quaker spirituality by themes from psychology, in particular, recently, from the 'personal growth' schools of thought. This involves a substantial shift in the Quaker understanding of human nature.

Throughout most of Quaker history this view of human nature has shared, despite important differences, much common ground with orthodox Christianity. These shared beliefs include the following: we are prey to all manner of sins - pride, hatred, covetousness, etc; these have to be resisted by divesting ourselves of the self-centredness which is their common feature and opening our hearts to what God would have of us; this will necessarily entail sacrifice; it is the narrow way, the Way of the Cross; yet, in the acceptance of that discipline lies true freedom because our real self is the self God would have us be.

Over the first half of the century or so, this pattern of belief was weakened by the new liberal Quakerism, with its roots increasingly in the secular and individualist ground of the times. This increasingly stressed the acceptance of our natural selves. Sacrifice and discipline, therefore, are suspect. Instead, self-expression is extolled. As for sin and evil, despite all the collective sins of the century, Friends developed a more optimistic view of the innate goodness of humankind. And the will came to be seen as an external authority which crushes our divinely natural impulses.

Several of my predecessors in the inter war years and the 1940's noted this trend and argued passionately against it. Francis Pollard - who was an achetypal Quaker liberal - does acknowledge that Christianity may have been too repressive in the past; but he is quite clear that *laissez-faire* or self-expression are quite inadequate bases for the educator unless combined with the disciplined tempering of the will.[18] Margaret Harvey, in 1942 regrets, for her part, that we have 'learnt from psychology more exactly what man is and [confuse] that with what he ought to be.'[19] In other words the evolution is towards accommodating religious thinking to the description of what humankind naturally is.

This development was already far advanced in the 1950s when I was growing up. I remember the awkwardness with which words like 'sin' were used, the sense that they were outdated. But it was taken much further in the 1960s with the emergence of 'personal growth'. In this term I include all those movements in the fields of psychology and counselling which are centred on the importance of loving oneself and nurturing one's gifts.

This approach sets little store on the will; sacrifice is dangerously life-negating; discipline is a strait-jacket; and anything which makes for guilt is to be shunned. Such terms are fast approaching extinction in BYM. Self-expression is all important. Nothing must be checked or criticised.

I do not suggest that personal growth philosophies have nothing to offer. The morbid negativity of some traditional Christianity needed to be overcome. I am also aware that feminist experience has been particularly receptive to personal growth, not least because it offers an alternative to low self-esteem and paralysing guilt.

Nonetheless, I do believe that an uncritical acceptance of such 'personal growth' positions is damaging to many of the Society's core positions. It is another part of the process which has led

BYM, as it moved closer to 'the world', to end up colonised by it. What are my criticisms?

Firstly the nurture of self can all-too-easily become an end in itself[20], which is an end to true spirituality. Secondly 'love' is an exercise of the will: we cannot just rely on love growing in us by giving free rein to our self-expression, by 'taking time for ourselves' and 'being kind to ourselves'. The self which we nurture, is it our self-willed self, or the Godself within? Thirdly, where is the gap between what we are and what we should be? It is not only that early Friends knew that gap and their power came from the expectation and the experience of crossing it; it is also that it is essential to spiritual experience. Without it we would never need to be forgiven.

Although personal growth philosophies have influenced us as a continuation of the liberal Quakerism of post 1895, in other ways the two are sharply opposed. The pride of place given to the rational is reversed in favour of personal experience, emotion and creativity. There is much talk about relearning god language; perhaps we need to renew our understanding of the virtues of the will to selflessness. Whatever the case may have been in the past, the world today is surely not suffering from an exaggerated emphasis on self-abnegation.

It is worth looking at one particular aspect of this trend in rather more detail. The question of guilt arouses strong feelings amongst us. Time and again voices are heard which reject guilt out of hand. At the Friends General Conference in 1985, Sonia Johnson expressed this contemporary horror with force:

> Women have been manipulated by guilt so massively that we are experts in guilt, and we will all agree that guilt is a useless emotion; it's negative and nothing positive can come from it. We must eradicate it entirely.[21]

It is often difficult to express guilt in Quaker circles because the taboo is now so strong. If one tries, reassurance is immediately offered. Once, having ministered about a particular failing in me with what seemed less pain than the message deserved, I was encouraged not to feel guilty about it. On the contrary, I should have felt more guilty, rather than less. By that I mean I should have properly felt the damage that my conduct had involved and deeply dedicated myself to its non-repetition.

It seems to me that we need to return to some robust common sense. If we accept ourselves as we are without reservations then guilt will not arise; but surely we cannot be as self-satisfied as that! If we do not see, or feel, any need to change our conduct, from where will the motivation come to change it? If we do feel the need to change our conduct in certain respects, then we are conscious of a gap between what it is and what it might be. Whether in our daily lives or in wider public questions, that gap is the spur to change. This is at the heart of religious experience and it is the source of the prophetic voice. It is that gap which creates guilt.

If that is so, there is no need to fear guilt. Only a need to receive it as a messenger of Truth and as such, informed with Love. Let me repeat. I know from my own experience that men have often imposed a more paralysing guilt on women, because I have done so; *that* guilt is not freely acknowledged as Truth informed by Love; it is imposed, often deviously, in a damaging exercise of power. Nonetheless, the essential experience of being convicted by the light cannot be forsaken without almost irreparable damage. Nor is guilt always paralysing. Certainly not to early Friends who expected the light to show them and change them and lead them away from temptation.

Why can we not share that experience? The reason, I believe, lies in the fact that we no longer experience ourselves as forgiven, because we don't believe in a God personal enough to forgive. Guilt, then, is only paralysing in the absence of forgiveness; forgiveness must have a source. We will not be able to encourage and challenge each other effectively over our lifestyles unless we can overcome this blockage. As soon as we try the barricades will go up around our self and we will lose sight of love, peace and truth in the desperate effort to avoid knowing that where we are is not always the place God or the spirit would have us be.

Sartre gives a powerful illustration of exactly this problem in his play, *Les Séquestrés d'Altona*. The play is about the absolutisation of history in a world without God. In other words, if there is no God, there is no Court of Appeal other than the verdict of the march of history. So, if our choices are not confirmed by history, we stand absolutely condemned. There is no appeal from the judgement of history when history is all there is. That is the outcome of a nihilistic and secularising culture. In which case there is no forgiveness and guilt is irremediable. As Friends, however, our guilt ought to be remediable because the God of truth is also the God of love.

The Cultural Climate: Conclusion

I have tried to show how the growth of relativism and of secularism has permeated BYM from the cultural climate of the age. These are large questions which have very practical implications for our individual and corporate faithfulness in living out our beliefs. Relativism fragments our understanding of what we are for and what we can do; it weakens commitment to anything: the gentle greys of spiritual and moral relativism are death to the prophetic; death, indeed, to any powerful leading. Secularisation saps our spiritual power and undermines our testimony to the sacramental nature of the whole of life. Accommodation with the times destroys our ability to judge them in terms of faith.

- Chapter 3 -
Context: MATERIAL CONDITIONS

Were all superfluities and the desire of outward greatness laid aside and the right use of things universally attended to, such a number of people might be employed in things useful that moderate labour with the blessing of heaven would answer all good purposes relating to people and their animals, and a sufficient number have leisure to attend on proper affairs of civil society.

John Woolman[1]

Friends' Changing Social Status
The social position of Friends today is not what it was in the nineteenth century when Friends were drawn disproportionately from the tiny upper middle class. Today we form - now in the lower reaches - a much smaller part of a very much larger middle class. Our collective experience is of sustained downward social mobility. I suspect that more of our members are in the bottom half of incomes than for a very long time.

Let me make this claim more graphic, though my figures are suggestive rather than carefully proved. *The Friend* in 1863 reported that the average income for every Quaker, child, woman and man, was £182, at a time when the average wage was £50.[2] Thus each Quaker had an income of three and a half times the average wage. A rough calculation suggests that we would each need an income of some £35,000 to maintain the same ratio!

How do we view this change? Many will say that our loss of financial power has caused the Society's financial problems. Our greater distance from the centres of power has also weakened our political and social influence. In the world's terms, the change has to be viewed as a loss. Spiritually, however, it may be a liberation.

We view our Victorian inheritance through rose-tinted spectacles - the great Quaker trusts are still at work with their chocolate names. The story of Quaker philanthropy is well-known. However, another story is slowly coming to light - of Quaker slave traders, of opposition to the Factory Acts, of ruthless repression of trade unions. The cause of the famous strike of the 'match stick girls' at Quaker-owned Bryant and May was the dismissal of workers suspected of giving information to Annie Besant for her exposure of the firm's dangerous practices, tellingly entitled, *White Slavery in London*.[3]

The plain fact is that Victorian Quakerism wore the narrow blinkers of its social standing. Its merit and its fault was philanthropy. The causes it took up were at a safe distance, like slavery, or generated benevolent feelings of superiority, such as alcohol or gambling. The only cause which touched the economic system as such was the gospel of free trade, which was held to benefit the working classes by driving down prices. With honourable exceptions such as William Allen, there is little understanding of the oppression of the working class. Hence, while Friends contributed £1000 to the anti-slavery movement in Bradford in 1833, only £3 went to the factory movement.[4]

Quaker hypocrisy in this respect was demonstrated by exposing the gulf between its concern for black slavery abroad and its neglect of 'white slavery' at home. Elisabeth Isichei quotes from *The Poor Man's Guardian*: 'But the white slavery of Englishmen suits the Quakers; they continue to have houses built for them, and to enjoy all the bounties of Providence ... Let the Friends show a sympathy for the white slaves of England.'[5] She also quotes the cry of the chartists to J.J. Gurney: 'Think of the slaves at Home'.[6]

The picture is even darker. When Quaker industrialists and politicians were given the opportunity of the Factory Acts to limit their exploitation many opposed them. John Bright, for example, termed Fielden's Ten Hour Bill, 'one of the worst measures ever passed'.[7] And J.T. Ward claims that 'both Bright and Ashworth tried to defeat its intentions, in their own factories, by means of a shift system.'[8]

Opposition to and ignorance of the class struggle went hand-in-hand with class prejudice. The Adult School Movement created a problem for Friends as its members were from much 'lower' social strata. How should they be integrated? Would they be encouraged to apply for membership? Elisabeth Isichei shows convincingly that they were kept at a distance, quoting one Friend's views: 'Do you wish to invite chimney sweepers and costermongers, or even blacksmiths, to dinner on Firstday? Do you intend to give their sons and daughters a boarding school education?'[9] That this was no aberration is confirmed by the Manchester Conference of 1895. It includes Kenerie Ward's moving account of Quaker snobbery when, after a life of poverty, he discovered the Society of Friends but was virtually ostracised by his Meeting.[11]

The degree to which Victorian Quakers' spirituality was corrupted by their social position should be clear. Too many of them had too much to lose and, unlike John Woolman earlier, they were unable to transcend their class interests.

By 1930, the Society of Friends was transformed, and largely liberated from paternalist benevolence. It was renewed not only by its acceptance of the modern world intellectually but by being freed from its upper middle class blinkers. By the 1920s London Yearly Meeting was earnestly debating the social order and affirming the need for fundamental change. For example, the Committee on War and the Social Order, albeit ahead of some Friends' thinking, minuted in 1918: 'Holding the view that capital is largely the accumulated surplus of common human effort, we believe that its possession should not entitle any class to exercise control over the lives of others.'[11]

Such thinking abounds in the years between 1910 and 1940. But we have not developed it. Our social witness has marked time as we have been unwilling to face awkward issues or dream visionary dreams. Our contributions have been piecemeal and reformist compared with those of interwar Friends. The reason is doubtless that middle class Friends at the turn of the century drew on the energy of rebellion against the limitations of their upper middle class inheritance. Our problem is that we are too cut off from all those who are most exploited and diminished by a social order which confirms our comfortable, middling status. That must be one of our starting points.

My other starting points are just two of the many directions in which Britain is being rushed along: first, inequality; and second, consumerism. Both raise major questions for our faith.

Inequality

> It is in exchanging the gifts of the earth that you shall find abundance and be satisfied. Yet unless the exchange be in love and kindly justice it will but lead some to greed and others to hunger.
>
> Kahlil Gibran[12]

We have a testimony on equality, with offshoots on hat honour, titles, slavery, gender etc. All these are grounded in our conviction of the essential equality of all as equally children of God.

When I was growing up, that testimony appeared to be in the process of realisation. The world seemed to be moving, albeit against powerful resistance, towards the emancipation of one oppressed group after another: slaves, colonial peoples, women and, to an extent, working people. Indeed much was done to increase equality for many sections of the population. The Welfare State seemed like the realisation of the dreams of Friends in the 1920s and 1930s: a liberal democracy with universal social provision. Apart from its foreign policy, it seemed close enough to the Kingdom for Friends to identify with its values.

Some of these trends have proved to be extremely powerful and have continued into the 1980's and 90's - for example, the vital movement towards a fuller sense of gender equality, as well as that which has furthered the liberation of the lesbian and gay members of society. But in other respects we have witnessed or undergone an historic reversal of a century old trend towards greater equality of wealth and income. The forces that have inflicted this defeat on our testimony to equality should not be restricted to those unleashed by Conservative Governments since 1979. The international dimension suggests a wider process is at work. Nevertheless, British governments have generated inequality much faster than most countries.[13]

This theme can be illustrated in many different ways. One of the most telling is the percentage of the population living on below half the average income. In 1977 this was about 7%; by 1990 it was three times larger at 21%. Relative poverty on such a scale has not been seen at any time since the Second World War. Moreover the gap between the low and high paid is at its widest since 1886.[14] Tellingly, Oxfam decided in 1995 to include the U.K. in the list of countries where it works, to be followed by the Tear Fund in the following year..

How has this inequality been created? The answer lies in the following measures:

- INCOME TAX CUTS FOR THE RICH AND SUPER RICH.
  These cuts gave an average £33,300 a year at 1992-93 prices to the top 1% of earners and an average £400 to the bottom 50%.[15] The combined effect of changes to direct and indirect taxation in the decade from 1985 boosted the top tenth of incomes by 6% and diminished the bottom tenth by 3%.[16]

- HUGE INCREASES IN PAY AND PERKS AT THE TOP END.
  Paul Foot gives the example of the £545,000 clear profit Roger Allwood, Finance Director of Mirror Group Newspapers, gained from the exercise of share options in 1995.[17] By 1993 the top 10% of incomes averaged £45,397. The bottom 50% averaged £7,794, or 17.2%, compared with 23% in 1980.[18]

- THE LOWERING OF THE TAX THRESHOLD IN REAL TERMS.
  Employees start to pay income tax at 23.8% of average pay compared with 36% in 1979.[19]

- THE CREATION OF LARGE SCALE UNEMPLOYMENT.
  This is both the cause of a considerable part of the increase in poverty and of the increase in the social security budget, which has then led Ministers to argue that the Welfare State can no longer be afforded.[20]

- THE ENCOURAGEMENT OF LOW PAY.
  This was done by measures which weakened union organisation and particularly the right to strike, which scrapped the Wages Councils and put Local Authority and government services out to tender, etc. There has been an increase of 25% in the proportion of employees in full time work earning less than the decency threshold set by the Council of Europe.[21] 70% of all new part-time jobs are for 16 hours or less and do not offer employment protection, or holiday or sickness pay.

- SOME SIGNIFICANT REDUCTIONS IN BENEFITS.
  Notably for students, young people and those who are sick or unemployed etc.

- STEEP GOVERNMENT-GENERATED INCREASES IN RENT LEVELS IN BOTH HOUSING ASSOCIATION AND COUNCIL PROPERTIES.
  The latter have doubled in real terms since 1979.[21] Housing Association rents are now so high that few tenants get a significant financial benefit from working.

- THE LIMITATION OF STATE PENSION INCREASES TO THE RATE OF INFLATION RATHER THAN THE RATE OF WAGE INCREASES.
  It is now only worth 15% of average male earnings and this is likely to drop to 6% by 2040.[22]

- THE IMPOSITION OF VAT ON FUEL AND THE INCREASE IN THE STANDARD RATE OF VAT.

Some Friends seem to think this hardly matters. Poverty is relative, they suggest, and as such is not really real. I believe this view to be a fundamental error. If poverty were absolute or nothing, a British family of five living in a three roomed house without television, fridge, washing machine, carpets, car, newspapers, never eating out or taking a holiday and only able to afford an absolutely basic diet, might be said to be poor. But, if they had any of those things, then not. Under such a definition, if the Conservative Government's decision to increase pensions in line only with prices rather than incomes was continued for fifty years and the pension was worth less than 10% of the average wage, the pensioner would not be considered poor. As Shipley Brayshaw succinctly concluded in 1932: despite the 'speed with which luxuries become necessities ... the fact that the boundary line is shifting and elusive should not prevent us seeing the essential facts.'[24]

What relative poverty points to is the effect of inequality. And, although Friends have never developed a corporate testimony to complete equality of incomes, they have a testimony to the vital importance of equality, not only as a spiritual reality but as needing to be embodied in social and economic arrangements. Equality of opportunity is not enough to fulfil our testimony: in conditions of gross material inequality equality of opportunity is a sham: real opportunities remain starkly unequal - as the mortality statistics demonstrate all-too-clearly. Gross inequalities of wealth and income result from, embody and create grossly unequal power, which is incompatible with the testimony to equality and, in turn, compromises democracy. Finally equality of esteem is impossible to achieve in the wider society in such conditions; those with least are esteemed less: council tenants less than owner occupiers, cleaners less than managers. In short, this reversal of the development towards greater equality can only be understood as an attack on the essence of Quakerism.

There are other ways of becoming aware of injustice than statistics. Stories need to be told. Just consider Jean and Roy, who have had debt problems since the last recession. They are on full rent and keep on paying a bit off the arrears; then something crops up and sets them back to square one. Her job as a barmaid in the local pub was stopped while it was closed following gang violence. He works as a cleaner, one job on a morning shift, another in the evening. Twice the doctor has signed him off work with back problems; each time he has found that he would get deeper and deeper into debt as the Housing Benefit would not be immediately adjusted and his sickness benefit would be far too low to cover the rent in full. So he has struggled back to work against medical advice. There's no holiday pay either. He's already lost a job once by taking a holiday and finding 'his' job had been given to someone else. *The Government has reduced sickness benefit and reduced job security.*

There's Bill, a redundant older worker who has found a security guard job at £2.20 an hour. It's an hour by bus to work and an hour back and the shifts are twelve hours long, which makes a fourteen hour night. His earnings are low enough to need topping up with Family Credit. *Low pay has been one of the signal achievements of the series of Conservative Governments over the last sixteen years.*

At a Church Action on Poverty meeting a young woman told us her story of living in Bed and Breakfast accommodation. She was moved miles across London away from family and friends. The journey back to keep friendships alive was hard to make with the children and the cost was a very considerable part of her weekly benefit. The wall paper was hanging off in strips in the damp room. There was nowhere to go and little to do. Understandably she became depressed. *The Government has decimated the supply of affordable social rented housing.*

However, inequality is created by the combined effect of the changing standards of living of poor and rich. It is the gap between. It is not so much that the poor have got poorer (though significant numbers have), but that the better off and the wealthy have grown much richer. The gap has been enormously widened, particularly by the top 10% of incomes which have disappeared almost out of sight. More and more people live in comfort and more and more in luxury. There are ever more stories of people doing up houses to very high standards - adding second bathrooms, jacuzzis, swimming pools, conservatories; of children being taken from ballet lesson to piano, from cubs to horse riding; of those buying holiday homes and yachts; of those who spend more on a meal out than many have to spend for a whole week. Many of them are educated expensively in the private system, and increasingly they buy in health care. They are fitter and live longer than those who are poor. Moreover, the brazen self-interest of today's wealthy lacks the civic consciousness that bestowed an aura of virtue on Victorian wealth.

This growing gap is our challenge. Will Hutton indicted the middle classes as a whole in *The Guardian*: 'Just to identify the task underlies its magnitude - and the degree to which Britain's opted-out middle class has deserted ordinary people in its quest for self-advancement.'[25] Work has not been shared fairly; financial sacrifices have been visited on those least able to bear them and those who could easily have afforded to contribute more to the commonweal have refused to do so.[26] How far are we Friends caught in the net of Will Hutton's accusation? How have we responded to this polarisation of society in the last twenty years? Few of us have been amongst the greatest gainers or losers financially. We have also tried in a variety of ways to resist such developments. Many Friends have continued to shun the more conspicuous forms of consumption. Many have aimed at other rewards than the highest salary. Many have continued to live out their convictions on equality and simplicity. Apart from themes already mentioned we find Friends working on gender equality, gay rights, disability, employment opportunities, the benefits system and on new ideas for a Citizen's Income amongst much else. Without such work we could have no claim to the testimony.

We have clearly been leaning against the tilt of the world.

However, we have not managed to turn this individual fact into a unifying corporate stance against inequality. Locally, some Meetings set up Poverty Action Funds to redistribute unjustified tax gains to the wider community; some set up housing projects of different kinds; others have striven to raise the consciousness of their members on issues such as racism. We have, from time to time, also spoken as a Yearly Meeting on the iniquity of growing inequality, as with the Statement on Poverty at Yearly Meeting in 1987. No doubt many Friends also considered that their individual political involvement was an attempt to work against growing inequality and polarisation. However, was this enough? Did it amount to a message that, as a spiritual priority, London Yearly Meeting was corporately and actively working against the Government's adoption of measures which massively increased inequalities?

The highest profile resistance to the Government's creation of deeper inequality was the campaign against the Poll Tax. We can take it as a test case. That measure should have been anathema to Friends. In the context of a concerted attempt to widen inequalities it was the cruellest blow. Of course, there were those who gained from it and, in some cases, it was fairer. But, overall, it was thoroughly regressive. Yet, corporately, we had nothing to say.

There was concern. The issue dripped into the letters column of *The Friend* for over a year. One or two Meetings raised it, notably Lewes Monthly Meeting, Oxford Meeting and Young Friends Central Committee. But, without central work to focus the energy, it was dissipated. Quaker Social Responsibility and Education (QSRE) was paralysed - unnecessarily I now believe - by the received opinion that one waits for concerns to come through from Monthly Meetings.[27]

Corporately we shirked the Poll Tax because it was too political, because it involved defiance of the law, because it would have meant campaigning alongside militant political organisations like the Socialist Workers Party and Militant. We feared division and preferred not to ruffle any feathers. (Unlike Yearly Meeting, locally single opposed voices are often enough to block a Meeting's sense of unity.) Perhaps also, and most shamefully, Friends were not more involved because relatively few of us were badly affected and probably more gained. A minority of the letters to *The Friend*, indeed, extolled the virtues of the Poll Tax, warning us against opposition to 'a radical change which time most likely will prove to be a positive one'.[28]

We must stop assuming that God's will requires us to act in respectable ways, associating only with respectable people. We have developed a reflex against getting our hands dirty by joining with militant campaigns. Respectability is not next to godliness. The publicans and sinners were not respectable for sure and Jesus associated with them. Can our Peace Testimony only survive if we don't test it in situations of potential violence, including demonstrations where we are not in control of events? It would be a poor little testimony if it could not survive in a Poll Tax demonstration.

So, the defeat of the Poll Tax owed little to Friends, or the churches, or middle class pressure groups. It was achieved by the messy business of demonstrations which focused the widespread, intense hatred of the Tax and by the huge levels of non-payment, sometimes from principle, sometimes from need.

It has been easier for Friends to support the principle of fair taxation and to oppose the massive tax hand-outs to the rich. It involves mostly words on paper, rather than bodies in the street and the courts. Even so, we have rarely sought to make an impact with it. After the 1992 General Election the political debate moved so far to the right that conventional wisdom ruled out increases in taxation on anyone earning less than £50,000 or even in some cases £100,000. Per person! Even the former is over ten times as much as many people get on benefit. The rich in effect insist that it is more important for them to have two cars, a holiday house, the children's pony, personalised number plates, private schooling and the rest, than to make any further contribution to the community. This is egotism on an Old Testament scale.

. The obscenity strikes home when we remember that we don't have enough money in the public purse to keep class sizes under thirty, to house homeless people, to maintain our parks, or to prevent hospital emergency cases being trundled round the country looking for a bed. The theory is put about that we can no longer afford the Welfare State. Steps are taken to shift the responsibility to the individual to make their own provision, leaving, as with pensions, an increasingly poor residual safety net. But Britain spends much less than almost every other country in Europe on social security;[29] its pensions and its unemployment rates are also amongst the meanest. The only reason for cutting down on social provision is to appease those who want ever more to spend on luxuries.

So, where is extremism now? Do we want to carry on down the American road? There is a thrust in contemporary British society which would deny the validity of our testimony to equality. That attack may not be on our Meetings or on our physical lives and possessions. But is it not a real blow to the heart of our faith?

Let me return to Ordsall. It is a place with fewer resources than most. The gulf between it and affluent Didsbury is huge. And it has grown. The polarisation between the rich and the poor has been magnified geographically. In the poorest estates those who can afford to buy, move out and on. Those who are left are increasingly those who are unemployed or sick, those with fewest resources generally.[30]

Who is responsible for that inequality? I do not want to negate personal responsibility or local initiatives. But this gulf cannot be bridged by personal responsibility or local initiatives alone. Nor good will. Nor fine words. Society has decreed that places like Ordsall should group together those with few qualifications, limited financial resources, and, sometimes, little hope. It is a place where families often don't have the money even for subsidised trips, where central heating systems are often not used, where educational qualifications are rare. In the conventional use of the word it is a living 'testimony' to inequality. Such estates are not far away geographically, but they are another world. We are cut off from it as surely as were Victorian upper middle class Friends; in some ways more so as we no longer have the Adult School Movement. Our testimonies to equality as well as to peace and community are too rarely present where they are most needed.

Consumerism

> My money might say to me, 'You have enough to buy that,' but my God might say to me, 'I don't want you to have it.' Now, who am I to obey?
>
> Richard Foster[31]

Some years ago I went to pick up my daughter from a school trip. The arrival time was late and not too predictable. It was a sharp winter's night. I arrived and switched my engine off. After a while I got out of the car and paced up and down to keep warm for the hour or so before the bus arrived. Nearly all the other cars were still running their engines to keep warm. That memory has come to represent for me the temptation of ease: getting cold occasionally has been the human lot ever since we began. Perhaps all those gestures of swinging the arms and stamping the feet will soon have died out? We can avoid getting cold now and most of us do. However, I need to admit that I took our car; it was only a mile and a half; I could have walked. What am I prepared to consume for my comfort?

That may seem a trivial example. In itself it is. But it is also revealing of the way in which we become accustomed to ever higher levels of material comfort. And comfort, with its bedfellows, convenience and ease, is a very persuasive smooth-talking demon which often succeeds in sending our spiritual sense to sleep. Keith Helmuth warns us that this 'drive for maximum convenience' is leading to ecological disaster as well.[32]

Inequality is one of the forces which drives this process. The desires of us all for greater and greater consumption will be dragged upwards in the slipstream from the increasingly excessive affluence of the country's highest earners - some would say robbers. (The tell-tale 'some would say', despite all the authorities for that position from the church fathers and Woolman to Marx, underlines the power of the middle-of-the-road.)[33] The financially privileged - who pour scorn on trade unions for protecting differentials between skilled and unskilled work - conveniently forget that, as soon as the masses have acquired what was once theirs alone, they restore the gap with something more ostentatious and out-of-reach - the personalised number plate, the gold plated bath taps, the luxurious health cure. And, in turn, their new luxury products and experiences are fed into the imagination of the rest of us, to fuel our desires. Inequality, or relative poverty and acquisitiveness, are, therefore, integral to the capitalist system. Our desires are ratcheted upwards almost irresistibly.

This process of spiralling aspiration applies especially to expenditure on leisure. When I grew up our family holidays were mostly spent camping. We travelled by public transport to some remote spot - by which we meant the MacGillicuddy's Reeks or Craig-y-Nos rather than Nepal. Even so, most people could not venture so far; many not at all. Now, while there are still significant numbers for whom tourism is a day out in Blackpool, for the rest the urge is to travel ever further and colonise the remote places all over again, this time by force of money rather than arms. Tourism is the world's biggest industry and its impact is enormous whether we consider the 'sex industry' in the Far East, the ruined beaches in Europe or the multiple forms of pollution everywhere. Do we consider that impact before we embark? How does the motivation relate to the spirit of acquisitiveness? Is 'seeing more' any better than 'having more'?

What does the consumer society imply about human identity? Its message is that it is neither 'being' nor 'doing' that counts, but 'having'; we are what we have. In our generation shopping has become one of the major leisure activities. As Archbishop Carey commented on the 1992 General Election campaign: 'one got the impression ... that the purpose of life was shopping.'[34]

Jeremy Seabrook has frequently brought his critical insight to this theme, for example:

> In the West, the buying of things (and indeed, services, experiences and sensations) has become inextricably bound up with the roots of human identity. We seek to express who we are through our purchases; and, at this point, the process of buying and selling ceases to be a mere mechanism, but comes to give purpose, and even meaning, to our lives.[35]

This stress on having cannot be squared with any account of faith. If our ultimate sense of value depends on our purchases, this breaks our link with God. For to worship wealth, which has no ultimate value, is to worship a false god, which is idolatry. In whatever ways we are possessed by our possessions we are separated from God.

The system, then, is based on the generation of ever more diverse wants. Its massive advertising industry is dedicated to this end. J.K.Galbraith has written a shrewd allegory on the theme:

> Were it so that a man *sic* on arising each morning was assailed by demons which instilled in him a passion, sometimes for silk shirts, sometimes for kitchen ware, sometimes for chamber pots, and sometimes for orange squash, there would be every reason to applaud the effort to find the goods, however odd, that quenched

his flame. But should it be that his passion was the result
of his first having cultivated the demons, and should it
also be that his efforts to allay it stirred the demons to
ever greater and greater effort, there would be question
as to how rational was his solution. Unless restrained
by conventional attitudes he might wonder if the
solution lay with more goods or fewer demons.[36]

Galbraith's solution of 'fewer demons' is in the great Christian
tradition which shows how self-centred desire breaks the true
relationship with God. Simplicity means essentially to be free
from entanglements; covetousness is sin. Earthly desires should,
therefore, be restrained not sated. The acquisitive society is a
sinful society and the essence of capitalism is incompatible with
Christianity.

Galbraith goes on to ask whether the market meets people's
needs or first creates them? Certainly the system could not work
if people did not want what they are offered. As he writes:

One may marvel at the attractions of often frivolous and
dispensable consumer artifacts and entertainments in
our time, but their ultimately controlling appeal cannot
be doubted.[37]

And yet, is that 'controlling appeal' the result of the genuine
exercise of free choice?

Later on in the same essay Galbraith recognises that,

In fact, the consumer is very substantially in the service
of the business firm. It is to this end that advertising
and merchandising in all their cost and diversity are
directed.[38]

The system persuades us that we freely want what in fact it
needs us to want. Rather than freedom, our behaviour has the
characteristics of addiction. Moreover the powers of persuasion
are exercised not in the interests of truth but through all manner
of distortion.

In either interpretation we are faced with daunting tasks. Either the whole population needs to be persuaded to want less and differently, starting with ourselves. Or we have to change the system which provides so much which people feel they want, even need - even if they really don't.

In the area of consumerism we have to begin with ourselves. How do we dissent from the encouragement of ever greater consumption? Much of this is associated with 'discretionary spending' - in other words expenditure that we don't need to make. Here is some of my very ordinary experience.[39]

The sale of refreshments makes ever bigger demands on most people's disposable income. This is one of the fastest growing service industries. However, on train journeys and the like it's still sandwiches and flasks for me. It's just a way of saying to myself: 'I don't need an income big enough to buy a cup of tea every time I go out.' This saves packaging too.

Rather more important has been my bicycle. I'm really fortunate that I've never had to drive to work. I try to use the bike whenever possible. Even if it's not convenient, if it's raining, if I have an early train to catch, if I'm tired and only just got back home. Excuses are just too easy - I know as I succumb to them all too frequently. I also know that the car eats up space, creates horrendous problems of air and noise pollution, large numbers of deaths and injuries, the destruction of habitat and dependence. I want to distance myself from that in a small way.

What is our response as Friends? Some are working in pressure groups and direct action campaigns to improve public transport and curb roads expansion; and some are putting their concern into practice - often much more faithfully than I manage: giving up the car altogether, using public transport whenever possible, even if it is more expensive. But I suspect that most of us are hoping for government action to curb the use of cars before we do much about it ourselves.

This position is miles away from a testimony. It surely should be seen as a spiritual issue for us all, rather than a question of waiting to be pushed into action by government. After all, cars kill large numbers of people as well as contributing to people's ill health and premature deaths. Every time we get in a car we decide that the particular end in view (going to Meeting!) justifies the means which I have just described. We may decide that it is justified on occasion, but not without question. If we took all those decisions in the light we would, I am sure, turn this worry into a testimony.

For me the hardest part is the assumption that hospitality demands the offer of transport, even when perfectly good alternatives are available - 'I'll run you home'! When I travel up to London - as I frequently do - Emily wants to run me to the station and to pick me up. She knows it would save me half an hour in the early morning or that I'm tired on the way home and it's a way of expressing her love. Yet, I'm content to cycle and feel it's right - usually. But, in my turn, I find it very difficult to deny that expection in my children and find myself running them home, where, if it was me, I would have gone by bus. This is an example of family egotism.[40]

Am I right that such decisions are taken in a thoroughly secular way by most Friends - as many others are by me? If that is so, then we have ceased to believe that all our decisions need to be held in the light. Yet, we say that the whole of life is sacramental. Do we mean it? Unless we do, our efforts to develop our spirituality will wither.

These are just a few of my little ways of creating a critical distance between myself and the values of the market. For me, each of them is a spiritual practice; every time I am in the position of thinking shall I use the bike or the car I am testifying to who I am and, through that, testifying to something which lies much deeper than my material advantage or comfort. Those decisions, whether I'm faithful or whether I succumb to convenience or whim, are the stuff of prayer. Every such tiny decision, taken in the light, reclaims the world of secular, routine practices for God.

Capitalism and the Market

> Capitalist ideology bites deeply and corrosively into our daily lives. It came as part of that package which we bought so unquestioningly ... It entwines itself with our feelings, winds its way round our affections, distorts our deepest needs, colours our whole conception of ourselves and of our human purposes, disfigures even our dreams. How we are to disengage from it must be at the centre of any discussion about alternatives: not as theory, but as the toughest and most intractable of material realities.
>
> Jeremy Seabrook

The presiding context of our religious life is the power of the market within a modified capitalist economic system. As we have seen, the capitalist market is based on inequality and generates it; and it necessarily fosters a materialistic consumerism. We need to be aware of the pervasive influence that this structure has on our life for good and ill. It has proved enormously successful in increasing the range of goods available to ever larger numbers of us, particularly in the advanced post-industrial countries. Now it appears almost unchallenged as the way of organising economic relations within countries and internationally - the alternative model attempted by the Communist bloc has failed.

Is the capitalist economic system an unalterable 'given'? Some have seen the liberal, democratic, capitalist system as the last word of social evolution. However, no system remains dominant for ever. However hard it is to think beyond the global market, we are right to insist that there will be such a 'beyond'. But this only matters if we believe that the system is not in tune with our spiritual values and, therefore, needs to be transformed. This is the crux. Do we believe it?

Until recently the worst excesses of capitalism were being slowly modified in the direction of greater social control and less inequality, through progressive taxation and the welfare state. Despite the core of systemic injustice, it was possible to believe the direction of change was compatible with our beliefs. Over the last fifteen years the changes have been largely reversed. We should be clear that the system is opposed to almost all our core values:

● It concentrates wealth and power in few hands. It is, therefore, incompatible with our testimony to equality.

● It exploits the power of money over human life, sometimes in very naked forms. If market conditions suggest that the factory is shut and relocated elsewhere, that is done, often with little or no thought for the human consequences. Profit is all.

● It generates poverty and inequality. It requires a reservoir of poverty because the gap between the rich and the poor creates the aspirations for greater consumption. There need to be many left behind in relative poverty. It necessitates both unemployment and low pay since both are required to increase profitability.

● It encourages a materialistic approach to life; everything is measured in terms of wealth, fame and power; we are encouraged to covet people and things; we are persuaded to define ourselves in terms of our possessions. Almost all of us spend more daily time absorbing advertisements than we do on any form of spiritual discipline. Covetousness is at the heart of the capitalist dynamic; its rejection is at the heart of Judaeo-Christian spirituality.[41]

● It is based on a thoroughly competitive philosophy, rather than nurturing the co-operative well-springs of our God-givenness.

It is possible that the system could be modified again in the direction of greater fairness and equality if there was the political will to do so - and it would require a very settled will. However, it is difficult to see how the materialist and consumerist bases of the system can be modified completely without the system itself being replaced. It is hard to imagine how the system could be made compatible with a fundamental equality.

This presents us with a very big challenge as we rarely consider the economic system as such: we may talk of poverty, of inequality, of materialism. But the system is too big, and, perhaps, too political. And, indeed, we may not have an alternative blueprint, and without it we are caught in two minds. Perhaps what we need is to honestly acknowledge our uncertainty about the exact shape of a society which would match our values and testimonies, as well as about the steps needed to move towards it. At the same time, however, we have to expose the gap between our values and this idolatrous system, idolatrous because it is worshipped as the unchangeable fact of our lives. That's why it was good to see the contribution of the Quaker Socialist Society to Labour's debate on Clause Four.[42] It reminded us that, even if the Labour Party converts to the market, there is something about its working which is fundamentally at odds with our deepest spiritual insights. Whatever our uncertainties about alternatives, that needs to be said.

- Chapter 4 -
A 'PEOPLE OF GOD'?

It is likely that our theological problem in the Church is
that our Gospel is a story believed, shaped, and
transmitted by the dispossessed, and we are now a
Church of possessors for whom the rhetoric of the
dispossessed is offensive and their promise is irrelevant.

Walter Brueggemann[1]

Society, Movement, Church, People

I now draw on material from the preceding chapters, focusing it
on the question: what is the Religious Society of Friends for? As
Margaret Heathfield expressed it:

> Is our Yearly Meeting a People of God, the Body of Christ
> as described in Paul's letter to the Corinthians ... or a
> religious organisation which is content to make its
> spiritual method available for those who are attracted
> to it?[2]

Until we know what we are, we cannot know what structures
will help us. What, then, is our model of being a 'church'?

We are not happy with any of the terms used for religious
groups. We are not a people in the sense that the Jews in the Old
Testament were. We do not see ourselves as a church, with its
credal, hierarchical and evangelistic implications. We are not
dynamic enough to be a movement.

Most Christian denominations differ from us in that they situate
themselves within the universal Christian Church, whereby the
message of Jesus is to be carried to the world. Their sense of
belonging has the three elements of local congregation, national
church structure and universal church, the last of which links
them to the ultimate meaning and purpose of life. The diagram

below, one of a number which illustrate different models of 'being church', is taken from Margaret Hebblethwaite's *Small is Beautiful*:[3]

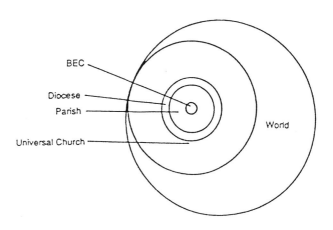

This diagram reveals the problem for us Friends. We generally have close bonds with our local Meeting; in addition many have a strong sense of belonging to a Quaker framework over time and space. But fewer of us identify with the universal church. Instead we relate to a much broader and vaguer religious quest in humankind as a whole. This state of mind is open-ended and exploratory rather than missionary or teleological. No wonder the dynamic word 'mission' is alien to us. If the 'good news' is only my good news, sharing it will have little priority. We do not easily see ourselves as bearers of a truth that others need; instead we offer a means of approaching spiritual exploration for those it suits.

In so far as relativism, individualism and easy-going tolerance are our hallmarks our message will be muted, both to others and also to ourselves. John Punshon detects 'a tendency for contemporary Quakerism to become a needs centred movement with an essentially harmonising and reinforcing role in the lives of its members,' as opposed to a challenging and transforming role.[4] This compressed quotation brilliantly sums up the effect on our faith when the transcendent vanishes and leaves us as we are, with our needs and our desire to feel at peace and to be confirmed that 'I'm all right'.

Our Problems with Corporateness

Our sense of what we are defines our approach to the corporate. A loose collection of free-thinking individuals will certainly not become 'a people of God'. It is, indeed, arguable that the individualistic temper of contemporary Quakerism leads to a dominant mood of introspection, despite continuing arguments which we hear against our supposed over-emphasis on outward action. Inevitably this mood will seek a disengagement from corporate Quaker expresssion of faith.

This surfaces in a variety of questions: is the financial crisis a sign that Friends identify solely with their local Meetings? do we let into membership people who just want a club for mutual support? are we so divided that it would be impossible to reach agreement on anything? First, why do so many Friends today jib at the corporate?

Relativism, Individualism and Secularisation

I have already shown how the climate of ideas has made it much harder to think in terms of the Religious Society of Friends being a people obedient to God's will. The more our faith is reduced to individual preferences, the more truth appears relative, the less possible it is to envisage corporate action.

Corporate purpose is also weakened by a spirit of acceptance of the world as it is. I have already argued that the spirit of accommodation to the world has become more dominant during the twentieth century. This is Neave Brayshaw's reaction:

We have now to understand that the way of Christianity may involve a separation from the world, not some artificial marking of itself off as in itself good ... but the separation of the pioneer minority who break with the world's conventions if these are hindering them, who suffer loss of friendship and good standing.[5]

There is little evidence that London Yearly Meeting took that message to heart. Rather the spirit of accommodation grew stronger and the attacks on corporate action more strident.

The Understanding of Membership

Relativism and individualism, in turn, affect our understanding of what it means to be a Quaker; instead of discipleship, membership can seem to involve little more than belonging to a cosy spiritual club. Alastair Heron, in his studies of attenders and newly joined members, shows that many are most attracted to Friends by the friendliness and support of our Meetings. The Society's role is to provide a welcoming, non-judgemental space for individual spiritual journeys in all directions. Is this purpose enough?[6]

Our Business Structures

Our current business practices also stifle corporate concern, turning us inward rather than outward. Our insistence on discussing everything in meetings to which all belong ensures that too many people spend too much time discussing insubstantial administration while the pains of the world and the concerns of Friends are hardly addressed. We have scarcely begun to recognise this for the profligate waste of our time and energy that it is. If only we had listened to Henry Hodgkin over sixty years ago:

Too large a proportion of our thought seems to be needed for keeping the machine moving ... leaving too little free energy for getting out into the world with a word to deliver.[7]

But we cannot listen because we treat the whole of our business procedures as sacrosanct, rather than the essential spirit of our business method alone.

The Political Implications of the Attack on the Corporate

These are some of the factors in the weakening of our sense of corporate purpose. However, they have a larger social and political context. In brief, many middle class Friends disparage the corporate because they fail to understand that justice has to be struggled for. That struggle is necessarily corporate. To minimise Quaker corporate action is to say that Britain Yearly Meeting can be faith-full while washing its hands of the injustices with which it is surrounded. It is easy to leave the individual to her or his own fate only if you take a relaxed view of what that fate is.

Let me illustrate this by taking Dorothy Nimmo's exposition of the position. She claims that the individual's power is usurped by the corporate, which should, therefore, be minimised; and that the intention to 'make the world a better place' is overweening pride and should give way to a less oppressive approach of saying: 'We are going to let the world be as it is.' And she draws the conclusion:

Perhaps there is, can be, no such thing as the work of the Society. There is only the work of each individual Friend...[8]

This recalls Margaret Thatcher's famous comment: 'There is no such thing as society'. Both assume that all that is worthwhile starts and finishes with the individual. Therefore, the less the individual is subject to wider powers the better. Dorothy Nimmo adopts the extreme historical pessimism which argues that, because humans make mistakes and we cannot guarantee that our social policy will be for the best, we will do least harm by standing by and letting things happen. One thing is certain: this offers absolutely no countervailing power to that which dominant groups and institutions exercise over the individual. Implicitly it accepts the prevailing inequality of power. And, where there is no offsetting institutional power, we know the truth of Tawney's words: 'freedom for the pike is death to the minnow'.

An individualistic rejection of the corporate is a classic middle class world view. Nothing suits the established powers better than to dissolve groups into their component individuals, who are then almost helpless against them. This can be seen in many contexts. Take the Conservative attacks on the Trade Unions: employers now regularly dismiss people without cause or notice; as isolated employees, often not unionised, they have little redress.

Unlike the working class, the middle class did not need to acquire the virtues of solidarity in struggle or the virtues of struggle itself. Friends are tempted by the middling place they occupy in society with its - erroneous - assumption that they can and do look after themselves. But faith is corrupted if it neglects those on the margins. Despite Dorothy Nimmo's plea, corporate power will continue to exist. The only question for us is whether we allow it to operate unhindered or whether we seek to use our influence corporately for justice and truth. The impact of our abstention might be only small, but it would surely be negative. Indeed Liberation Theology challenges us to ask ourselves whether we can properly be a Christian people unless we are with them and their perspective is at our heart. Are we? Is it?

Finally, if we were to banish issues of corporate social responsibility from our business meetings, how much harder would it be for them to be faced boldly in our worship. Quakerism would have been cut off from its history of social concern, divorced from its bedrock in the sacramental nature of the whole of life. The shattering of Truth into myriads of individual opinions would have moved from the realm of theology into the realm of testimony. All that would be left is our shared practice of silent worship. It is doubtful whether the Society would survive on that basis. Ben Pink Dandelion has shown how crucial a cohesive factor, in the absence of unity of belief, is Friends' shared sense of social values.[9]

The Rediscovery of the Corporate

The question for BYM lies deeper than the dilemma over corporate and individual emphases in our current practice. It is rather whether our coming together to worship brings us into glimpses of Truth which we need individually for our journey towards God and which the world also needs for its wholeness. Otherwise corporate action will seem arbitrary and inessential when the language of priorities is spoken. Does our faith, then, cast light on society in ways which convince us that the light is not mere subjective preference?

If we look at it from our understanding that there is that of God in everyone, we know at a very deep level that God is being oppressed and humiliated by society's maltreatment of so many of our brothers and sisters. For example, those whose 'economic worth' is least are persuaded that they have little value; those who live in fear-ridden urban deserts; those crippled by asbestosis in the name of profit; and so many others.

If this criticism of the social order is more than a rationally argued political choice or mere personal preference, if it is discernment through our faith values, are we not under a spiritual imperative to live it out in our corporate life, as well as individually? That is what our testimonies should help us do. As we practise them, they become a means for building up our corporate life. Rediscovered and practised more deliberately they could recreate a corporate Quaker identity, a sense that, together, we have been given something vital to do.

Corporate Unity through our Testimonies

Some Friends at this point may suggest that I am being naive. Surely, they will say, if we cannot agree on our beliefs, we are unlikely to agree on the implications of our testimonies, which involve contentious economic and political issues. Far better, they will go on, to leave the individual Friend to act; corporate unity on questions of social order is impossible.

Such views, which are not uncommon, are siren calls, out of our individualism and relativism. In their defeatism, they imply that, even if individuals still put their faith into social action, Friends corporately could say and do nothing about peace and poverty, sustainable development and anti-racist work. The basis for testimony would have been destroyed.

I know full well that reaching corporate unity on social problems will be no simple matter. I do recognise that not all Friends see eye to eye on everything! We do not agree about Quaker schools, the right to strike, abortion and much else. But we should start from testimony, not policy. Let's take the example of unemployment. Our starting point is our testimony to equality. On that basis we will share a conviction that unemployment in general is unjust: it is a way of sharing work and income that is radically unfair. We then need to discuss our differing perspectives on how the problem is to be tackled.

Some may emphasise long term changes in the organisation - and understanding - of work; others may argue that work should be more fairly shared now, through a variety of expenditure and taxation proposals. But it can be a dialogue on common ground.

We need to remind ourselves again and again that the highest and deepest realities of human life - which are of God - are crushed all around us, and sometimes in our hearts too. With deep unity at that level, attitudes towards particular policies will become more manageable. Sometimes we will reach unity; sometimes we will fail; sometimes our differing proposals may rightly coexist. But our starting point must be unity through our testimonies.

Consider the Peace Testimony. Differences of opinion exist amongst Friends on the Second World War, the Gulf War, the use of sanctions, UN peacekeeping forces, liberation struggles etc. Nonetheless we have the testimony and a clear corporate approach to issues of peace and war. Quaker Peace and Service is able to act corporately on our behalf even if not every Friend is in agreement.

Friends are no more divided on truth or equality or simplicity than they are on peace. I believe we are broadly united on the following propositions, for example: inequality should be reduced through taxation and benefits policies and raising low pay; there should be greater openness in government; ever harsher penal policies are not only ineffective but wrong; car usage should be discouraged. It would be wonderfully strengthening if we learned to approach social problems on the common ground of our testimonies, so that even the differences stand out against a common backcloth.

If the serious practice of our testimonies could reinvigorate our corporate life - as well as our spirituality - how can this be brought about? We cannot rely on the prevailing currents of society. They are flowing in an opposed direction. However, many Friends are paddling upstream in all sorts of craft. The beginning is to become more aware of that and to celebrate it. Then we need to reflect on our testimonies and discover ways of sharing our successes and our failings as we strive to witness to them. In terms of this chapter I offer reflections on mutual accountability, re-evaluating concern, on discipleship, and on rediscovering community as approaches to being more 'a people of God'.

Mutual Accountability

Our individualism prevents our learning from each other. We could ask those who have practised simplicity, those who have done without the car etc. to share their spiritual practice with us. But we are afraid of such sharing - it might make demands on us. We claim to be open to God's guidance, but we close up if it comes through that of God in another Friend. We have not created a culture of mutual encouragement and of keen stimulation. We need to develop not just a culture of disclosure but of mutual accountability. There are numerous ways of doing this, of which I shall outline just two, since the difficulty lies much more in the wanting to do it than finding the ways to do it once the desire is there.

The first has been part of QSRE's *Rediscovering Our Social Testimony* exercise. Friends could be asked to share their experience of living out our Testimonies, in the hope that we would be drawn towards the insights of each other. Such a meeting might end with Friends being asked to say what possible implications for them they wish to take away to prayerfully work on.

A second approach is to take our faith seriously enough to review it annually with some other Friends. Such a meeting would be broader, looking at our lifestyle as an expression of our faith and a sign of our spiritual condition.

The exact approach is of less importance than the recognition that most of us cannot successfully keep the powerful forces of the market at bay on our own.

Testimony, Concern and Corporate Concern

Friends have developed a very particular way of approaching social witness. It places overriding priority on the individual under concern. The 1986 Report, *The Nature and Variety of Concern* in particular, distinguishes the true individual concern which

94

impels a person to a particular - and probably costly - course of action, albeit with the support of the Quaker community, from a 'concern about' an issue such as homelessness, where the hope is that a corporate body of Friends will say or do something.

These two approaches to concern are certainly very different. True individual concern is very vivid. It partakes of a world where guidance shapes our life in ways which would not have been chosen by self-interested reason. Like pacifism, it bears the stamp of the absolute in a relativistic age. Corporate concern about an issue works very differently, by gathering elements of concern from many, creating a common spiritual understanding of the issue and inviting many to respond in often quite small practical ways. It is the democratic face of contemporary Quakerism, whereas the individual concern is an important survival from our theocratic origins.

Corporate concern has been made to seem distinctly second-rate. Because it is less costly than individual concern it is seen as less spiritually valid. Because there is no hard and fast dividing line between what Deborah Padfield has called 'a bother'[10] and something deeper some Friends seem to be close to believing that we should shun it altogether.

We would be poorer and less serviceable if we did. A deep corporate sharing of concern about the world is an exercise in discernment and the beginnings of prophecy. What we are offering is our vision, drawn from the silent depths of worship, and given into the arena of social struggle. Our influence may be small; our voice may often be very slow to be heard and sometimes fallible. But can there be any doubt but that the world needs to hear the voice of other values than those of success, power and wealth? I would plead for a new understanding of the importance of our corporate concerns. Imagine BYM without a concern for truth in public affairs, without its tardy critique of the lottery, without a place for reflection and action on homelessness! That would cut us off from the real world, impoverishing both ourselves and it.

Far from cutting ourselves off, I see the need for plunging in more actively and with fewer glances over our shoulders to weigh up the impact on our reputation. I share Henry Hodgkin's plea to Friends in 1933:

> we seem to be on the verge of forgetting that all the great causes of God and humanity must be fought for in the market place where men rub shoulders with one another, and by persons who will take off their coats and get right on with the job.[11]

Integrity from the sidelines is too easy; integrity in the political maelstrom is the challenge.

Testimony offers a key bridge between individual and corporate concern. The relationship between the three aspects of our witness can be illustrated through the example of BYM's concern for housing. Some Friends will be working in the field under concern: some, for example, will have moved house, as we have, led to embody our testimony to equality in this way. Many more, however, will have taken other forms of action, working away on soup runs, in campaigning organisations, on management committees of special needs housing projects and so on. Their action, which may not count as a fully fledged concern, is not without its cost. The line between 'acting under concern' and just living out our beliefs is far from hard and fast. What BYM's corporate concern does is to gather up and refocus all that spiritual energy from all our attempts to put our testimonies into practice. The aim will be to encourage better national policies and more faithful Friends. In this case, for example, it may encourage Friends to pray about housing, to work on their lifestyles, or to participate in the political education work of the Churches National Housing Coalition.

Let me summarise my understanding of the relationship between these three elements in our Quaker life, the individual concern, testimony and corporate concern.

An individual concern is an individual or small group under concern, carrying through a piece of work which results from a direct calling.

Testimony is the corporate working out of our faith in the concrete world; from time to time particular actions to express our core values of peace, truth, equality, simplicity, community become necessary to our spiritual life.

A corporate concern - for housing, against racism, or whatever else - is a position adopted by the Society to try to move our own lives and the political process in the direction of our testimonies. It needs to be grounded in the lives of Friends who have worked actively on the issue. It looks towards limited forms of action from large numbers of Friends. For example, I was involved in raising the question of sexism in St Andrews Meeting and then through East Midlands of Scotland Monthly Meeting before sending it through to London Yearly Meeting.[12] I see no essential difference in the spiritual process involved in that from the various actions I have been led to under individual concern.

The danger of overemphasising the traditional individual concern is that it is relatively rare in its pure form. As such it is an unhelpful standard for the generality of our corporate Quaker decision-making processes.

The danger with corporate concern is the opposite one: we could easily have more than we could manage. Issues might be raised to which few Friends had devoted their energies. However, the danger of misuse is no reason for rejecting it. If we were to exclude such corporate concerns it would leave a void, for many Friends, at the centre of the Quakerism they want to practise.

We should also rethink our understanding of the testing of concern, whether individual or corporate. The traditional method of testing through Preparative and Monthly Meetings can work splendidly when those Meetings are live. But they are sometimes dead. They may even be dead in the midst of live corporate concerns going on outside them. The vital thing is that the concern be real and be thoroughly tested. Sometimes a corporate concern may be apparent in a diffused form throughout the Society and we should be able to test this, perhaps through Representative Councils, rather than rigidly insist on the letter of the traditional process.

We should also expect to develop work on the basis of our testimonies. When I started work as Clerk of QSRE I assumed that, whilst we could continue existing work, new work would have to wait for a Monthly Meeting to raise a specific concern. It was all right to keep on doing new pieces of work on criminal justice because it had been a Quaker concern for so long, but we should not think of working on the Lottery because no Monthly Meeting had sent minutes and there had been no central work on gambling for some time.

But that was, surely, too narrow. QPS does not wait like that. It responds to new issues as they arise, with the Peace Testimony as a continuing guide. Similarly QSRE should be helping BYM discern how our testimonies can be brought to bear on contemporary social problems. If that had been the case, the diffuse concern about the Poll Tax, coupled with our understanding of our testimony to equality, might have allowed for creative work on the issue before it was too late.

I have stressed the importance of corporate concern as the focusing of our energy on a particular social issue where our testimonies have something to say. I now go further. I believe that it would be right for us to consciously develop a role of speaking from corporate concern, pressing for the realisation of our testimonies in the world. It would be hypocrisy to preach the Kingdom of God without striving to bring it about. Part of that striving, in conditions of mass democracy, must be to bring our sense of ultimate values into the political market place. We cannot be faithful to our ultimate ideals unless we wrestle with their incarnation in a pretty messy world.

Discipleship

That means taking seriously the role of disciples, as we call the followers of Jesus. But can we, if we no longer see our faith through the life and death of Jesus? If not Jesus, whom or what do we follow? For discipleship is a following after; it suggests that there is a model of life which is calling us to 'take after' it.

Is there nothing else which can make disciples of us? Can we not be disciples of the living God? Of the divine light, within and beyond? I believe we can, indeed must. If it is our experience that there really is that of God in each one of us, is that not in itself an invitation to us? To cherish it in ourselves and others, rather than snuffing it out? How can we take heed of the promptings of love and truth in our hearts without following them? Surely we can be disciples of the divine light. If our Meetings are to be more than clubs, if we are to meet the challenge of living against the times, we need that dynamic sense of discipleship.

Community

But, above all else, it is in strengthening our practice of community that we will fit ourselves to be more truly a gathering of disciples in the world. Community is a neglected testimony. It is particularly relevant to a world in which individualism and the free market have broken down so many solidarities:

> Today there is not much evidence of any kind of community, and for the lack of it war is waged in our hearts, and on our streets, and in our world.[13]

Community is an antidote to the cult of the individual and the worship of individual success. The extent to which we are able to practise it is a sign of how seriously we take the challenge of individualism to our faith.

Some may find this emphasis strange. They may say that Friends, more than most, are already in community. I suspect that the degree of community in our Meetings is quite problematic. It is sufficiently strong for unresolved hurts to loom large enough to drive people away; it is insufficiently strong for those hurts to be often enough healed. It is strong enough to create ties of friendship, but not strong enough to challenge us into more faithful discipleship.

The major influences on my thinking here have been Parker Palmer's *A Place Called Community*[14] and Elisabeth O'Connor's books on the Church of the Saviour in Washington.[15] In the Church of the Saviour membership requires discipleship. People give the core of their time and energy and money rather than what is left over after other needs have been met. They join even if it means moving their homes and jobs. The church is built in community. Community is a place close enough to deal with the hurts and misunderstandings which crop up along the way. It means

> staying locked in a concrete, given web of relationships until we come to know ourselves as belonging to one another and belonging to the Body of Jesus Christ.[16]

Emily and I once explored whether such a community could be created amongst British Friends. A dozen or so Friends from Manchester met over several months. We explored possibilities of an intentional urban community as well as ways of being community within a Meeting, perhaps as a grouping like the Iona Community. But the group was not led in either direction and eventually disintegrated, but leaving one other household and ourselves to make separate journeys into different parts of the inner-city. I suspect that it was not so much political differences that fragmented the group as differences of belief, or age! There were also strategic differences in our approach to discipleship and the corporate!

We both still yearn to be part of a more committed community. Such a community would not only be close enough for the combination of loving support and loving challenge which Quaker Meetings often cannot reach, it would also necessarily be an active, outward facing community of disciples, what Carl Heath called 'A society of doers of the word'.[17] Can this be done within the individual Meeting? If not, is there a role for a new 'order' of Friends who share the discipleship commitment?

Can we reach further towards that? Community becomes much more real in shared vision and action than it can be through mutual friendship. The fourth discipline of the Church of the Saviour was:

> Be a vital contributing member of one of the confirmed groups, normally on corporate mission.

They discussed laying down this condition, 'pressed by busy people'; but they reaffirmed it:

> We were never able to conclude that we could have a community in Christ by signing our names in a book, subscribing to the budget, and coming to church on Sundays.[18]

I am more and more convinced that Friends would be more effective if we moved from our present structures for business to a more active format of groups with particular remits. There is a dead weight of routine business that is done because it always has been and it saps our energy. Why not expect all members to be associated with a team: Education and outreach; Social life of the community; Housekeeping; Peace and social witness. Plenary Monthly Meetings would be less frequent and would have two main functions: to review the work of the groups and to consider major issues.

More recently I have come across an illustration (overleaf) of the kind of approach I favour. Once again it is drawn from Margaret Hebblethwaite:[19]

Further on she describes a church with a similar approach, the Lakewood Catholic Parish in Colorado. It has six Action Ministries: Growth (including worship and religious education); Social Events; Assistance; Transition (people moving in and out); Stewardship and Administration. There is a gap in the area of social witness, of which they have since become aware. Stewardship is particularly interesting. The Stewardship group meets every household once a year to review its use of time, treasure and talent. If we flinch, is it the individualism of our age in us?

BEFORE   NOW

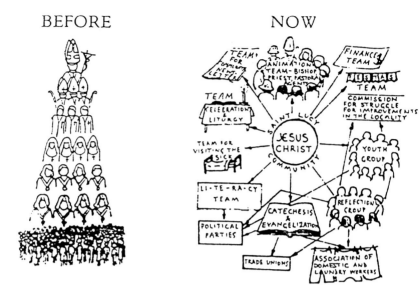

Conclusion

Are we, then, a 'people of God'? In part, of course - though how much more so we could yet be. A people of God is a community on the move trying to discern and follow God's word for themselves and for the world. *Discernment, Discipleship, Testimony* and *Prophecy* are key areas for our reflection.

A Quaker community, defined as bodies of non-dogmatic disciples of God's love and truth, resolved to follow the individual and corporate leadings given to them, expecting to be tested and changed through that process and determined to live faith out in the world of social struggle as well as in personal relations and in lifestyle - that would be a wonderful adventure. And nothing hinders it except the will.

How much remains to be done can be gauged by our response to the following piece from R.H.Tawney's *The Acquisitive Society*:

> 'He hath put down the mighty from their seat and hath exalted the humble and the meek.' A society which is fortunate enough to possess so revolutionary a basis, a

society whose Founder was executed as the enemy of law and order need not seek to soften the materialism of principalities and powers with mild doses of piety administered in an apologetic whisper. ... It will appeal to mankind, not because its standards are identical with those of the world, but because they are profoundly different. It will win its converts not because membership involves no change in their manner of life, but because it involves change so complete as to be ineffacable. It will expect its adherents to face economic ruin for their principles with the same alacrity as, till recently, [*sic*] it was faced every day by the workmen who sought to establish trade unionism ... It will voice frankly the judgement of the Christian conscience on the acts of the state, when to do so is an offence to nine-tenths of its fellow-citizens ... it will have as its aim, not merely to convert the individual, but to make a new kind, and a Christian kind, of civilisation.[20]

- Chapter 5 -
SIGNS OF HOPE

A new heart also will I give you, and a new spirit will I
put within you: and I will take away the stony heart
out of your flesh, and I will give you a heart of flesh.
And I will put my spirit within you and cause you to
walk in my statutes.

Ezekiel 36: 26-27[1]

Signs of Hope in Britain Yearly Meeting

I have focused on a small number of large social problems and
some serious weaknesses in our Friendly ability to respond to
them. I do not apologise for concentrating on these. The global
market will not be quickly transformed and proposals to create
greater equality nationally or internationally will meet enormous
resistance, against which even a corporately united BYM would
seem puny. Yet, I would not be writing this unless I could hope
for change. Unless we believed that our faith values were
applicable in the real world we would have to adopt a dualist
approach which separates the kingdom and the world. It is our
holy foolishness to continue to believe that love and truth are
not unattainable ideals but can be progressively revealed in our
hearts and embodied in our institutions.

When the Churches National Housing Coalition (CNHC) was
formed, a housing concern was actively circulating through the
veins of Yearly Meeting, even before being 'recognised' at Yearly
Meeting in Warwick in 1993. QSRE's housing group at the time
had been reformed with a specific remit to enable Friends to make
links with the Coalition. CNHC itself recognised the
disproportionate role of Friends in the Lobby of Parliament in
December 1993. Quaker Meetings were also represented far in
excess of their numbers in the church bodies affiliated to CNHC.

For all the joking about the slowness of Friends' business methods, we can see here the wonderful directness of our 'transmission' through our structure, because of our size. It is also a good example of Friends being ready to engage in such political activity without more ado because we share this sense of working to overcome the causes of social evils.

We may also be critical in some respects of Friends' delayed response to the National Lottery which the government has recently introduced. However, it is a cause for celebration that Friends have been in such close unity on it. The National Lottery has overwhelming support from the population at large most of whom play it. For Friends to be so clear in their opposition suggests that in very significant ways we are non-conforming to the values of the time. This should encourage us to expect such unity when our deliberations are based on our fundamental values.

Our guarantee that hope is, indeed, realistic is given by our own personal experience of resistance. Many of us Friends are struggling to lead simpler lives and few of us drive flashy cars even when we can afford to. Many of us have opted out of the rat race for success and wealth in significant measure.[2] In our business method we still practise a form of dialogue based on truth rather than power. For all our blindspots, active Friends are putting faith into practice to a significant degree. (I can say this after having been so relentlessly critical.)

Yet there is nothing very special about us. Nothing. Whatever the extent of our faithfulness, nothing inherently prevents anyone from becoming aware of and following the direction of the light within just as far and faithfully. We have no special gifts in that direction; it is not a matter of intelligence or reason and there is no spiritual gene. This, then, is our hope: the true self, which is of God, can always be discovered in everyone; that true self will always lie beyond self-interest and will always seek the good of all. Regardless of our theological formulations we agree on this Quaker 'universalism'. Hence my belief that the motivation for our outreach should not be based on the need to keep the numbers up to fill the vacant positions and the empty coffers. Rather it should be based on two beliefs: that Quakerism helps some people to find that of God within them, which will change them; and secondly that it will augment the power of love and truth in the world, which the world so sorely needs. I am prepared to say that Quakerism encourages movement towards the Kingdom. If there were more of us that movement would be stronger.

The possibility of this discovery of that of God within, even in the least auspicious circumstances, has been vividly evoked by our Friend, Bob Johnson's work with high security prisoners in Parkhurst prison. The violence and self-hatred are worked through:

> They are burning away the dross that obscures and distorts, the trappings that disguise the true humanity of people, and they are revealing the true gold buried at the heart of every human being, if we can once make contact with it.[3]

It is true for us all. There is always true gold to be discovered, in us as in others. And every discovery of God within is a moment of change and a glimpse of the kingdom.

Signs of Hope in Society

Governments do not control directly all social developments though they may influence them. In some areas of life, where their recent influence has been less marked, substantial social progress has continued. Government may have increased inequality of income, but elsewhere the movement towards greater equality has developed in ways which Friends should be able to celebrate. Let me single out the movement toward greater equality between women and men.

The Liberation of Women

Women have gained confidence and have been more prepared to assert their independence when faced with oppressive relationships, refusing to simply serve the needs of a male partner without thought for their own aspirations and desires. Their educational attainments have outstripped those of young males. Household roles are shared also more equally and it is gradually less unusual for the male partner to stay at home and look after house and children. Clearly, that is not the whole story. Women form an absurdly low proportion of MP's, of top civil servants, judges, managers etc.; physical and sexual abuse of women is still all-too-common; women's pay rates are still much lower than men's. Nonetheless, here is a story of liberation in progress.

It is a story in which Friends have a chequered part. With our initial emphasis on equality of men and women, the Society should have been much more to the fore. If it has often not been, I suspect it is because the living testimony has been overlaid by conventional values. Pam Lunn has shown how the Society shamefully failed to support the campaign for women's suffrage in the early years of this century.[4]

More recently we have had opportunities to acknowledge the importance of gender equality for Friends. The issue was on BYM's agenda in the 1970s and 80s around the time of the very significant 1986 Swarthmore Lecture by the Quaker Women's Group: *Bringing the Invisible Into The Light*. The reaction from Friends was mixed. Too many Friends had been too convinced for too long that equality between women and men had been achieved within the Society of Friends for them to imagine that there could be more truth on the issue.

We needed to know that gender relations even amongst Friends have been unequal and distorted for all their apparent parity. I believed that my relationship with Emily was one of equality. I started off married life as house husband; I played my part with the children and the household and the rest. I was the 'new man', apparently. Everyone said how lucky Emily was to have me as a partner. That sense of achievement was the cause of my blindness. For all our happiness there was in Emily a deep distress.

It took years for me to see that my relationship with her was also destructive:

> I came to understand that my childhood had been an apprenticeship in hiding the emotions, in self-sufficiency and intellectual supremacy: I was rarely at a loss for an argument; I rarely lost an argument. And so, in the guise of truth and intellectual rigour, I could control crucial decisions in our life together, or, more insidiously, the apportionment of praise and blame between us; my appreciation of Emily's musical, visual and poetic gifts, though genuine, was insufficient 'compensation'.[5]

When I came to see this through Emily's periodic pain, and through wonderfully enlightening discussions in St Andrews Meeting and East Midlands of Scotland Monthly Meeting I also came to see how damaged I was also by my stress on intellectual prowess. I believe that there are thousands and thousands of damagingly unequal relationships between men and women Friends, which have not yet been brought into the light. For example, my grandmother, Mary Spence Watson, as a young woman, was an active speaker on the great issues of the time, like women's suffrage. I would never have known that. My memory of her is of a quite private woman who ran the household while her husband, Francis Pollard, led the life of a very active 'public Friend'. I cannot help thinking that some of her gifts were sacrificed.

That seems less surprising if, as I recently have, you read through virtually all of the Swarthmore Lectures before 1945. You will be dumbfounded by the sheer quantity of the sexist language that they contain. I cannot believe that any of us would write like that now. In reading them we are drenched in the assumption that the world is man's. If I am right that none of us would write like that now, the polarised positions that have been taken up need revising. I suspect that we have all changed, but that some of us have not yet realised that we have. And, therefore, that further change may be needed.

I can understand this as I am still resistant to the loss of both the hierarchical and sexist language for speaking about God as 'lord' and our promised land as 'the kingdom' as well as the metaphorical inheritance of the imagery of light and darkness - which is problematic within an anti-racist aspiration.[6] Such transitions are awkward, we all recognise. I may lapse still into sexist language, but the awkwardness has disappeared from my use of inclusive language; the awkwardness is in receiving sexist language. In the end, the transition need not be awkward for long and is liberating.

Our Yearly Meeting structures have adopted inclusive language. Our new *Quaker Faith & Practice*, apart from historical extracts, has been rigorously monitored to ensure its language is inclusive. Yet I do not remember BYM corporately adopting a testimony against the use of sexist language as a part of its testimony to equality. I believe it would have been better to have done so explicitly rather than to let it quietly emerge. As it is we have a testimony by implication only. We could celebrate it much more effectively if we had worked our way through to adopting it as a group.

Sexual Orientation

Progress towards equality is equally decisive in terms of sexual orientation. Once again there is, of course, a very long way to go. But the situation has been transformed. It is not just a question of the rights that have been won, albeit not complete, in terms of the expression of sexuality, it is more the existence of a strong and self-confident people who cannot be ignored and who force the heterosexual community to recognise them.

I only have to think back to my first Quaker encounter with this issue in the 1970s in St Andrews, when the Minority Rights Group asked to hire our Meeting Room. For me, it was an issue perceived through ignorance and fear. We did eventually agree to the request despite some hard opposition. We have been greatly helped in this matter by our practice of openness and our commitment to the loving acceptance of each other. In particular we have been given the experience from those who have suffered from the discrimination. David Blamires' book, *Homosexuality from the Inside*,[7] was particularly important in helping us to overcome initial prejudice. Although the ignorance and fear are still in our midst, there is less now than there was.

Environmental Protest and Direct Action

Very different signs of hope have emerged in public concern for the environment. There has been a huge growth in the membership of environmental organisations and a major increase in the land under their control or management. The political influence of these rather passive memberships has not yet been maximised in many cases. But the roads protests and the animal liberation movement have both made an impact which is difficult to ignore.

My initial reaction to the protests against the export of live animals was to be amazed; but also disgusted that there should be so much more concern for veal calves than for people made homeless or forced into unemployment. But it was also impressive to see many people deciding that there were more important things in life than their own comfort and well-being and that the global market gives no-one a divine right to follow the superhighway of profit regardless.

Elsewhere we have had similar direct action over roads, both against the construction of new roads and to protest against high levels of pollution. These protests have involved participants both in significant risk and in breaking the law. Some Friends have been involved. I wish more of us had. The mobilisation of public opinion against the insatiable demand for more road space for more cars seems to have been given a huge boost by these actions.

There is a tremendous well of support for these issues and, I think for the methods adopted, which may be confrontational but are for the most part non-violent. Yet some Friends have reservations, I suspect. It will be said that there is no need for such action while we live in a democracy, and can make our views known through normal campaigning and voting in elections.

Democracy cannot, I believe, be limited to conventional campaigning and elections. It has to embrace forms of action which focus attention on a group's intensity of feeling, in addition to counting votes or opinions. In any case voting will not usually tell us precisely what people want because it involves a bundle of policies. So, for example, it is reasonable for a local community, insensed by inaction over road danger, to bring attention to their demands by walking backwards and forwards across a road and closing it for a while to traffic to draw attention to their grievance. Boycotts also, once seen as incompatible with the Peace Testimony, are now, rightly, familiar forms of action for Friends.

Of course, recourse to direct action should not be an automatic reflex and the methods adopted need to be appropriate. Nonetheless, in conditions where the centralised power of government is enormous and the domination of a narrow range of acceptable opinion is almost absolute, I would argue that most of these forms of direct action are signs of hope. We should consciously support them and encourage Friends to be open to this different form of service.[8]

But beyond all of this there are clear signs of a diffuse growth of environmental awareness which involves an enormous range of endeavour from energy production from renewable resources to the use of tropical hardwoods from managed plantations only, from the avoidance of animal-tested cosmetics to the development of low energy homes. And much else. Environmental constraints may well prove one of the most potent forces for change. If the relatively uncontrolled exploitation of natural resources threatens disaster then controls have to be agreed. Just as the unregulated national economies of the nineteenth century created problems which cried out for regulation, so, today the problems created by global capitalism require international regulation. Friends could encourage thinking towards that end.

Changing Patterns of Work

The possibility of a different approach to work is on the agenda. It is true that we are still struggling with an old system in which large numbers of people are overemployed and several million others are unable to get paid work at all. Nonetheless we can now see the possibility of everyone working less. Large numbers of people are already choosing to do so by retiring early. Others, like my eldest son, work as much as they need to and take time off for childcare in a way which would never have occurred to me at that stage. But there is potential for the growth of a much more human approach to work, where quite different kinds of paid and unpaid work are encompassed by the members of a household.

The idea of a Basic or Citizen's Income would greatly assist this process. It would provide everyone with a basic living allowance, whether they were in paid employment or not. Employment would be remunerated on top of that basic income. It would encourage work to be seen as an optional extra to be tailored to particular needs and aptitudes and easily varied in extent at different times. The idea is not easy to introduce in a world of political realism. But, it should have great attractions to Friends: it encourages us to think that paid employment is not the end of life; it suggests that many will choose more time rather than extra money; it minimises means tested benefits with all their attendant problems of dependency and deception.

The Reform of Our Democratic Institutions

There are equally signs of hope in the area of our democratic institutions. Hope here is not based on recent experience which has been very negative. Central power has enormously increased and local government has been emasculated. Much of what devolution of power has taken place has been to institutions that themselves are scarcely accountable.[9]

However, there is a growing body of opinion that is seized of the need for major reforms. These would reconstitute or abolish the House of Lords, create more effective checks against governmental power and provide greater defence for the individual against the abuse of administrative powers. But, beyond these particular reforms, there is a concern to revive political dialogue, so that the important issues can really be discussed beyond the length of a soundbite. Tony Wright, M.P. has argued in *The Guardian* for a more open and diverse way of practising politics, as 'the current range of representative voices is perilously small'.[10]

Nor is this question of 'the democratic deficit' simply another separate issue. Will Hutton suggests that it is closely connected with the middle class elite's desertion of the commonweal in favour of 'private schools, pensions, health and even personal security';[11] once again we are reminded that democracy may require a minimum of equality if it is to work.

Democracy was at the centre of Friends' definition of progress in the first half of this century. They would be saddened to see its current condition. They would be straining to ensure that a Quaker voice is raised for much higher standards of political life in every sense. We have to encourage in political life the will to recognise truth and to speak in truth. It is a sign of hope that we have our Truth and Integrity in Public Affairs Committee active in this vital work.

Towards a More Ethical Market

There is much else. The concern for ethical investment has grown very rapidly and now offers a rich range of opportunities for investment which avoids involvement in some of the most objectionable economic activities. There are also far more opportunities to shop with a degree of ethical discrimination through the activities of Traidcraft and the 'New Consumer' etc. The first of the Out of This World ethical shops opened in Bristol in November 1995. If we want to put our money where our principles are we have no excuse for inaction. Alternative investment where profit is not the major consideration is also increasing continuously.[12]

A challenge to the conventional measurement of the public good by the growth of the Gross National Product (GNP) has also begun to gather momentum. The ludicrous assumption that more means better has worn thin, The fact that the GNP is increased if the rain forest is cut down and sold, even if a priceless 'asset' has been destroyed for ever, has encouraged alternative economists to begin to develop more realistic measurements of socio-economic progress.[13] Credit Unions and LETS Schemes also establish areas of activity which are withdrawn from the market place. Credit Unions are community or workplace organisations which allow money to be borrowed cheaply and, if more widespread, could make loan sharks a thing of the past. LETS schemes take parts of its members' lives out of the cash purchase economy into a world of exchange of goods and services using its own alternative currencies.

Grassroots Participation: The New Barracks Co-op

More personally, the New Barracks Tenant Management Co-operative where I work is an underpinning sign of hope. Tenant Management Co-operatives are groups of tenants who manage their houses on behalf of their landlord and are paid to do so.

Our Co-operative is quite small, just ninety one households. In inner city Salford, more specifically Ordsall, which has the sort of reputation for crime and vandalism that makes outsiders want to live elsewhere.

In what sense is it a sign of hope? Firstly because it really does make a difference to the quality of life in a place where that quality can be very easily destroyed by despondency and fear. Neighbour nuisance, litter and vandalism are all tackled continuously. Roughly half of all households are represented on one or other of the Co-operative's ten groups: which range from Finance and Repairs to the Toddlers, Gardening, History, and Craft groups. The involvement of large numbers of the tenants in the affairs of the Co-operative gives them a stake in their area and a sense of pride in their Co-op. This is a hopeful sign, showing how personal behaviour depends on the right structures: many tenants come to us after despairing of keeping their patch clean because nobody bothers; in the Co-operative, individual effort is maintained because it is supported.

It is also a sign of hope for me because I experience all the time the skills and abilities of those I work with. Society classifies them as 'the bottom of the heap'. Many of them are part-time cleaners. But they run the Co-op, convincing me that society has repressed so much ability in them that a more just society could release and denied them so many opportunities which many of us take for granted. This brings to mind a Conference on poverty. I was facilitating a small group and was taken aback when a couple of Friends started talking about poor people often being 'inadequate'. I remember feeling almost paralysed, not knowing how as a facilitator I could respond. I must have prayed and there came to me out of the silence with a force I have never forgotten: that if anyone can be called inadequate it is those like me who, with so many advantages of wealth and education, have made society what it is.

CONCLUSION

The money in your vaults belongs to the destitute. You
do injustice to every man you could help but did not.

Basil the Great[1]

Where are the Agents of Change?

The problem is not, in the end, how to imagine a better world,
nor where to find signs of hope. The problem is to find convincing
agents of change. For a very long time, particularly in the 150
years after 1800, radicals believed that the working class would
replace a society based on privilege with one based on equality.
Now the working class is more fractured and parts of it may be
persuaded that they have a vested interest in the status quo. It is,
therefore, harder to see where the dynamic can be generated to
change a system as powerful as global capitalism - unless through
a crisis in capitalism itself or from environmental catastrophe.
However, the struggle for justice cannot afford to ignore the
continuing and potential role of the Labour movement in it; all
the more so, because working class resistance to oppression is
an essential building block of social justice which Friends have
neglected to our shame.

Accommodation or Dissent

Society has regressed shockingly in the last twenty years or so in
crucial respects. Despite the triumph of western democracies since
the Second World War, the ideal of democracy has been
thoroughly tarnished. Governmentally inspired distortion of the
truth has been well documented in the Vietnam, Falkland and
Gulf Wars, for example. U.S. Government agencies covered up
radiation experiments which they carried out on civilians which
were no better than those for which the Nuremberg Tribunal

condemned the Nazis. We should approach government propaganda with a deep scepticism. The struggle for truth in public affairs is rooted in dissent.

Will Hutton, following the Labour Party's Social Justice Commission, catalogues the regression in terms of inequality: 'From dental care to diet, life expectancy to suicide, Britain is profoundly unequal and becoming more so.'[2] He goes on: 'But inequality and injustice are not accidents. They are the by-products of introducing the market principle deep into the economy and society.'

The poor and the vulnerable are under attack. Are we clear that Quakerism is, therefore, under attack in its proclaimed testimonies? Unless we face up to and struggle against the world's proclamation of the kingdom of self-interest our spirituality risks being irrelevant. I have tried to show that economic and social change today, in key respects, run counter to our testimonies. Dissent, therefore, becomes a necessity in lifestyle, in politics and in testimony.

Lifestyle

> Despite years of hype, as yet few members of the public have given up much for the environment. Unleaded patrol is one thing, doing without the car is another. Reading about endangered species is one thing, giving up the exotic summer holiday is quite another.[3]

Geoff Mulgan's sobering reflection applies just as much to us Friends. It is not that we are entirely unfaithful. But we are content to be a little faithful and to be so privately. We mostly lean in the right direction but leaning is a form of movement that resists going very far. Unless our spirituality struggles with the real changes in social relations which are imposed on us, it will be a shallow affair, however fine its words. This means putting our faith first and grappling with corporate accountability, discipleship and testimony.

Political Dimension

No religious body is in a better position to unite around its fundamental values, our testimonies, and offer them to a world which is more than ever deprived of radical vision. That is the distinctive contribution Friends could make. We could be of service if we faithfully contributed to the public debate, seeking out much more actively than at present opportunities to share the vision inherent in our testimonies. The Leaveners are a splendid example of that dynamic in one context. We may not all be actors but, with encouragement and support we could be more effective agents of change.

I expect to meet resistance from Friends for whom Religious Society and pressure group4 seem incompatible. Many are also very wary of public statements. Certainly we should speak when we are clear (which may not be when we are unanimous). Certainly we should speak out of the real experience of our lives and do our best to avoid the hypocrisy of calling on others to do what we have not been able to do ourselves. Certainly we should speak to our testimonies.

But speak we should. It is a question of need. Christians have been prepared to prioritise the spirituality of responding to the needs of the hungry by feeding them. Friends have for a long time declared that we also need to rid society of the causes of that hunger. That also is a need, although much less widely recognised as an equally important aspect of faith. But BYM has had long enough to grow up. We cannot practice faith other than fragmentarily if we do not recognise the crucial influence of national policy on how life is lived.

A decision to contribute more to public, political debate to do the small amount that a body like ours can do to encourage openness, fairness and the values which make for true community would also be an aspect of testimony. I cannot emphasis too strongly that for me this would be a deeply spiritual path. It could only be done in faithful unity by a people of God. It would be a further stage in the proper response of religion to the development of democracy.

Testimony

Testimony, I have argued is the key link between the preceding sections on lifestyle and politics. As well as between both and faith. Testimony is the way in which we express in our lives our understanding of what human beings are meant to be: loving, truthful, peaceful and centred not on self but on God and therefore the natural world and other people. It is because we have neglected it that we have allowed our faith to fragment, so that our corporate witness no longer seems to some essential to our spiritual quest. It is because we have neglected it that we are too diffident to believe that our lives are lived as signs to the world. The rediscovery of testimony is crucial because it is the place where individual and corporate merge, fusing together lifestyle and politics and faith.

In all of this we need more passion. Our method of worship and of conducting our business meetings encourages rhetorical sobriety. We are concerned to keep to the truth and not to let our mouths run away with us. There is much that is admirable about this - indeed it is a distinctive testimony in my view. But is there also a loss? Are we too cool? Too afraid to let our hair down? Too afraid to speak with passion? Too afraid to express anger? Could I minister in this manner: 'The Church should be ablaze with anger on this issue (housing and homelessness). I could cope with the Toronto blessing, the Latin mass, the impenetrable prose of Church unity proposals, the most intricate details of restructuring schemes, and (tell it not in Gath) singing hymns from *Mission Praise*. IF (fond word) they all somehow led us to a concerted and determined, a passionate and committed, a spiritual and theological crusade against the evil of homelessness.'[4]

Political ministry is impoverished in our Meetings. If it speaks out of passion it risks hurting some; if it avoids passion and uses the language of sober reason, it will be seen as secular. If our spirituality shrinks from the public world it will shrink into the diminished space of private experience, where it will be cut off from faith's vision of 'a peaceable kingdom'.

That is why we cannot be content with the individualistic and relativistic and fragmenting Quakerism of this time. It drifts on the times when the times are for resisting. It undermines our confidence in our coherence, often without good foundation. It weakens our corporate life. Unchecked, it could destroy our In understanding of faith in action. The spirit of 1895 has been betrayed.

For some Friends, there is no other way to community than the reaffirmation of the whole of the beliefs of early Friends. No other way to testimony. No other way to become a people of God. They may be right; but, if they are, we would need to change almost totally. I believe that it is possible to find in a contemporary less Christocentric faith all the spiritual elements which make for communal discipleship: belief in the reality of spiritual guidance both for the individual and the group; the conviction, therefore, that there is Truth at the source of all; the calling to let our lives be ever more informed by truth and love; the realisation that we are divided between worldly desires and the love of God and God's children, but that our truest joy lies in giving and not in grasping for ourselves; the belief that the values of the time are always under judgement from the light and life which is eternal.

Might we not, on such a basis, come to rediscover that we were a people with a call?

REFERENCES

Introduction pages 1-18

1. *A Place Called Community*, Pendle Hill Pamphlet 212, 1977, p.27.

2. *Being Together*, Margaret Heathfield, Swarthmore Lecture, 1994.

3. A fuller account of this group reflection and of Church Action on Poverty ACTS Project can be found in the *Christian Action Journal*, Spring 1993.

Chapter 1 - **Faith and Action** pages 19-42

1. *The Passion of Political Love*, p.33.

2. Quoted in Margaret Harvey's *The Law of Liberty*, Swarthmore Lecture 1942, p. 48.

3. *Sundry Ancient Epistles*, Mss vol. 47, p.36.

4. *The Sign of Jonas*, Harcourt, Brace & Co., p.268

5. *Journey Inwards, Journey Outwards*, Harper and Row, 1975, p.28.

6. James 2:14.

7. See Neave Brayshaw, *The Things That Are Before Us*, Swarthmore Lecture, 1926, pp.18-19 and Margaret Harvey, *The Law of Liberty*, Swarthmore Lecture, 1942, p. 17.

8. *The Friend*, 28th January 1994.

9. *Can Quakerism Speak to this Generation?*, Philadelphia Yearly Meeting, 1933, p. 17.

10. *The Social God*, Sheldon Press, p.82.

11. *Religion and Public Life*, Swarthmore Lecture, 1922,pp 20-21.

12. Canon Barry, quoted by Caroline Graveson, *Religion and Culture*, Swarthmore Lecture, 1937, p.19.

13. *The Salt and the Leaven*, Swarthmore Lecture, 1947, p.69.

cf. "The Inner Self is becoming God" in David Jones, 'Rekindling the Trinity', *The Friend*, 29 September 1995, p.1230.

14. Quoted in Henry Hodgkin, *Can Quakerism Speak to this Generation?*, p.23.

15. Isobel Grubb, *Quakerism and Industry Before 1800*, Williams and Norgate, 1930, pp. 5-13.

16. Minute 7, 'Priorities for Central Work', Meeting for Sufferings, 7 March 1992.

G. von Schutze Gaevernitz expressed a form of this state of mind in his 1930 Swarthmore Lecture entitled *Democracy and Religion*: 'Only new men will build the new society. There can be no conquest of the world without previous conquest of self, no social reform without self reform.' p.89.

John Punshon takes a different view in *Testimony and Tradition*, Swarthmore Lecture 1990, pp. 44-45.

17. *Christian Practice*, 1925, pp.133-34.

18. Douglas Steere, *On Being Present Where You Are*, PENDLE HILL PAMPHLET # 151, 1967.

19. *Journey Inward, Journey Outward*, p.28.

20. *The Things That Are Before Us*, Swarthmore Lecture 1926, pp. 19-21.

21. *The Law of Liberty*, p.64.

22. Quoted by Russell Brain, *Man, Society and Religion*, Swarthmore Lecture 1944 p.76.

23. Elizabeth O'Connor, *Journey Inwards, Journey Outwards*, p.144.

24. 16 December 1994.

25. Douglas Steere, *Gleanings*, The Upper Room, 1986, p.67.

26. Minute 5, 9 April 1994.

27. Penguin Books, 1985.

28. *Quaker Faith & Practice* 23.21.

29. June 19 1987, p.791.

30. *Worship and Social Progress*, Swarthmore Lecture 1945, p.28.

31. *Social Thought in the Society of Friends*, Friends' Literature Committee, 1939, p.5.

32. *A Testament of Devotion*, Thomas Kelly, Quaker Home Service, 1979, pp. 36-37.

33. As related by Douglas Steere in *Gleanings*, pp 66-67.

34. *The Salt and the Leaven*, Swarthmore Lecture, 1947, p.37.

35. *The New Social Outlook*, Swarthmore Lecture, 1918,pp. 11-13.

36. *Social Thought in the Society of Friends*, Industrial and Social Order Council, 1932, p. 59.

37. *America is Hard to Find*, SPCK, 1973.

Chapter 2 - **The Cultural Climate** pages 43-62

1. *The Persistence of Faith: religion, morality and society in a secular age*, Weiden McColson, 1991. (Reith Lectures 1990))

2. *Towards a Quaker Restatement*, The Bannisdale Press, 1945, p.14.

3. Félicité de Lamennais: *Essai sur l'Indifférence*, 1817 (my translation).

4. I particularly focused on 'individualism' in the talk I gave to the Manchester Centenary Conference 1895-1995 in November 1995. This has been published in *The Friends Quarterly* of April

1996. I have, therefore, put the emphasis in this lecture more on other aspects of the cultural climate.

5. Alastair Heron terms this second phase 'post liberalism' and dates it from Kathleen Slack's 1967 Swarthmore Lecture, *Constancy and Change*. See his *Quakers in Britain: a century of change 1895-1995*, Curlew Graphics, 1995.

6. 'A case of the Liberal's new clothes', *The Guardian*, November 4 1995, p.29.

7. Albert Camus, *Letters to a German Friend*, 1948, (my translation).

8. Timothy J. Gorringe, *Capital and the Kingdom*, SPCK, 1994, p.4.

9. 'Are we led by the power of God?', Extracts from a Q-Room epistle, *The Friend*, 28 April 1995, p.519.

10. *Capital and the Kingdom*, SPCK, 1994,p.5.

11. *Testimony & Tradition*, Swarthmore Lecture 1990, p.23.

12. Ibid, p.5.

13. *Friends World Conference Report*, 1937, p.8.

14. *Religion & Culture*, Swarthmore Lecture 1937, p. 19.

15. *Journey Inward, Journey Outward*, Harper and Row, 1975, p.2.

16. *Selections from the Works of Isaac Penington*, Darton and Harvey, 1837, p.2.

17. *The Undivided Mind*, Swarthmore Lecture, 1941, pp32-33.

18. *Education and the Spirit of Man*, Swarthmore Lecture, 1932, p.75.

19. *The Law of Liberty*, Swarthmore Lecture, 1942, p.18.

20. cf. Anthony Clare who comments on an American freshman's admission: 'I'm not in a loving relationship, Dr Clare, I'm still learning to love myself' in the following terms: 'And the

therapists are encouraging this attitude, telling people that their principal activity in life now, and for the foreseeable future should be coming to terms with themselves. And everything else must be subordinated to this end, or worse, used for it. That's utter corruption.' In Sally Vincent, 'The Elusive Self', *The Guardian Weekend*, September 23 1995, pp. 20-25.

21. Sonia Johnson was a feminist Presidential candidate; the quotation is from the manuscript of her address.

Chapter 3 - **Context: Material Conditions** pages 63-83

1. *The Journal and Major Essays of John Woolman*, Ed. Phillips P. Moulton, Oxford University Press, 1971, p.240.

2. Quoted by Elisabeth Isichei in *Victorian Quakers*, p.166.

3. Dave Hill, 'The dying of the light', *The Guardian Weekend*, December 10th 1994, p.40.

4. Elisabeth Isichei, op.cit, p. 247.

5. Ibid, p.284.

6. Ibid, p.296.

7. Ibid, p.246.

8. *The Factory Movement 1830-1855*, London, 1962, pp.411-12.

9. Ibid, p.132.

10. *Manchester Conference of the Society of Friends*, 1895, Headley Brothers, 1896, pp.87-89.

11. *Social Thought in the Society of Friends*, 1932, p.15.

12. *The Prophet*, Heinemann, 1964, p.44.

13. 'While the rich get richer', *The Guardian*, February 21 1995, p.12.

14. In 1886 the lowest paid 10% of manual workers earned an average 68.6% of the median. By 1990 this percentage had fallen to 63.7. See David Brindle, 'Gap between low and high paid now widest since 1886', *The Guardian*, 21 December 1990.

15. House of Commons Hansard, 19 June 1992, col. 689.

16. Larry Elliott, Patrick Wintour and Ruth Kelly, 'Tory taxes favour rich says study, *The Guardian*, February 9 1994, p.1.

17. 'Now Labour is the enemy of the people', *The Guardian*, November 20 1995, p.11.

18. David Hencke, 'Recession made top earners better off and cut income of poor', *The Guardian*, April 6 1994, p.2.

19. Michael White, 'Tax rises "hitting low paid harder than big earners"', *The Guardian*, September 23 1995.

20. The Welfare State is not unaffordable. The U.K. does not spend more than other countries on it, but less. It is a question of whether the money available is spent on private affluence rather than social need. See, for example, Will Hutton, 'Research defuses time-bomb view of welfare state', *The Guardian*, November 9 1995, p.15.

21. The decency threshold is set at 68% of average gross weekly earnings. See: Peter Hetherington, 'One third of Britons earn "poverty pay"', *The Guardian*, November 22 1995.

22. John Perry, 'Deprived and depraved', *The Guardian*, October 18 1995, p.9.

23. Ruth Kelly, 'No easy answers to 21st-century pensions funding', *The Guardian*, March 14 1995, p.15.

24. *Unemployment and Plenty*, p.76.

25. 'Healing community requires reform rather than rhetoric', March 27 1995.

26. I am aware that elements of the Middle Class have been forced

to experience the insecurity even of their position. Neither the housing nor the employment market can any longer provide full security to many of those who are normally comfortably off; the political implications of this unforeseen result of revolutionary conservatism remain to be seen. There is, of course, some potential for a rediscovery of solidarity with those whose insecurity is more permanent. See, for example, Will Hutton, 'Fear of the Future', *The Guardian*, October 30 1995, pp.1-3.

27. See my comment in the following chapter, p. .

28. J.L.Turner, March 18 1988, page 344.

29. Will Hutton, 'Forget austerity era - Britain's rich', *The Guardian*, October 16 1995.

30. See Anne Power and Rebecca Tunstall, *Swimming against the Tide*, The Joseph Rowntree Foundation, 1995.

31. *Money, Sex & Power*, Hodder and Stoughton, 1987, p.56.

32. *If John Woolman Were Among Us*, Argenta Friends Press (Canadian Quaker Pamphlet, no.32), 1989, p.4.

33. Apart from John Woolman's writings there is excellent material on ownership in *Mine and Thine, Ours and Theirs* by Thomas Cullinan, Catholic Truth Society, 1979.

34. Quoted in Norman Shanks, *The Place of Dissent in our Society*, (typescript), 1992.

35. *The Myth of the Market*, Green Books, 1990, p.11.

36. Quoted by Judith Solomon, *QUNEC Newsletter*, no.7 June 1995.

37. *The Culture of Contentment*, Sinclair Stevenson, 1992, p.8.

38. Ibid, p.134.

39. See my address to the Manchester 1895 - 1995 Centenary Conference as reprinted in *The Friends' Quarterly*, April 1996, for

a more extensive exploration of this area.

40. We should look at this in the same light as governs Woolman's approach to making one's will, and his doubts about leaving one's wealth to one's children. *See A Plea for the Poor*, chapter 7.

41. In a previous Swarthmore Lecture John Punshon wrote: 'It is covetousness with which simplicity has to struggle. "You shall not covet" says the tenth commandment, one of the most important standing orders in that strict spiritual discipline which Jesus says we must transcend if we are to enter the kingdom of heaven. What it amounts to is a resignation from the whole system of personal rewards and satisfactions by which people usually operate, not only money and possessions, but more subtle things like status, reputation and everything which flatters and distorts the ego. Simplicity is the cost of discipleship.' *Testimony & Tradition*, Swarthmore Lecture, 1990, p. 64.

42. 'The Clause IV Debate', *Quaker Socialist*, Spring 1995, pp.4-5. The Quaker Socialist Society's submission to the Labour Party included, for example: 'The alternative to the domination of our economic and social life by capitalism is an extension of common ownership and democratic control.'

Chapter 4 - **A 'People of God'?** pages 85-103

1. *The Land*, Fortress Press, 1977. This theme is also helpfully explored from the marginalised perspective of lesbians and gay men by Zoe White in *Preparing the New Age*, Quaker Lesbian and Gay Fellowship, 1995.

2. *Being Together*, Swarthmore Lecture, 1994, page 108.

3. Fount 1993, page 23.

4. *Testimony & Tradition*, Swarthmore Lecture 1990, p. 42.

5. *The Things That Are Before Us*, Swarthmore Lecture, 1926, p.47.

6. *Caring, Conviction, Commitment*, Quaker Home Service and Woodbrooke College, 1992, pages 24-26.

7. *Can Quakerism Speak to this Generation?*, Philadelphia Yearly Meeting, 1933, p. 41.

8. 'The Kingdom and the Agenda', *The Friend*, 1 December 1995, pages 1525-27.

9. 'Quakers and Social Justice', *The Friends Quarterly*, October 1992, pp. 160-170.

10. 'Commentary', *The Friend*, 30 June 1995, page 811. Diana Sandy has espoused the individual concern against the corporate concern - which she has described rather dismissively as 'a socio-political need' with particular consistency. See, *Holding Up a Mirror to the Religious Society of Friends*, compiled by Janette Denley and Gill Roylance, 1988.

11. *Can Quakerism Speak To This Generation?*, Philadelphia Yearly Meeting, 1933, p.47.

12. An account of this process is given in Section C41-50 of *Freeing Each Other: a Quaker Study Pack on Sexism*, Resources for Learning Group, s.d. (1986?)

13. Elisabeth O'Connor, *Journey Inward, Journey Outward*, Harper & Row, 1975 p.172.

14. Pendle Hill Pamphlet # 212, 1977.

15. These include: *Call to Commitment*, Harper and Row, 19 . *Journey Inward, Journey Outward*, Harper and Row, 1968, *Eighth Day of Creation*, Word Books, 1971.

16. *Journey Inward, Journey Outward*, Harper & Row, 1975, p.27.

17. *Religion & Public Life*, Swarthmore Lecture, 1922, p.76.

18. Elisabeth O'Connor, Op.Cit., p.169.

19. *Basic is Beautiful*, Fount, 1993, page 22.

20. Quoted by Duncan Fairn in *Quakerism: A Faith For Ordinary Men*, Swarthmore Lecture, 1951, pp 34-35.

Chapter 5 - **Signs of Hope** pages 105-116

1. Authorised Version of The Bible.

2. The Voluntary Simplicity movement in the United States, with its coinage of the term "downshifting", is something BYM could explore: see 'Volunteers for a new America' by Walter Schwarz, *The Guardian*, October 25 1995, pp.4-5.

3. 'A cave of living treasures', *The Friend*, 16 June 1995, p.759.

4. "'You have lost your opportunity", British Quakers and the militant phase of the women's suffrage campaign, 1906 - 1914', *Journal of Woodbrooke College*, no. 5, Summer 1994, pp. 7-13.

5. From, 'Lest a Lesser Light blind us to a Greater' in *Freeing Each Other*, Resources for Learning, undated (1986), pp. 15-16. I have given Emily her real name rather than the fictitious name of 'Sarah' which was required at the time.

6. See, for example, the very challenging issue of *Quakers and Race*, QSRE, Autumn, 1995.

7. QSRE, 1973.

8. Environmental Non Violent Direct Action in 1995 has included Reclaim the Street parties, the mining of MIchael Heseltine's estate for open cast coal, the occupation of St George's Hill by the Land is Ours campaign and 'critical mass' bike rides in the centres of many cities.

9. For example, schools, NHS Trusts, colleges etc.

10. 'Why diversity is a dirty word', *The Guardian*, Ocober 2 1995,

p.13.

11. 'Healing community requires reform rather than rhetoric', *The Guardian*, 27th March 1995.

12. These include the Mercury Bank, now (Triodos with its imaginative housing-linked scheme through the Quaker Housing Trust) Traidcraft, the co-operatives' organisation ICOF and its Scottish counterpart Employee Ownership (Scotland) as well as the Centre for Alternative Technology have all raised funds on the basis that people want to see their money well used and will forego part or all of the interest they could gain.

13. Some of these register two decades of decline by adjusting for such factors as crime and pollution. See Victor Keegan, 'At last quality begins to count', *The Guardian*, October 16 1995.

Conclusion pages 117-121

1. In *Mine and thine, ours and theirs*, ed. Thomas Cullinan, Catholic Truth Society, 1979, p. 9.

2. Will Hutton, 'A Society to Shame Us', *The Guardian*, July 20 1993.

3. 'Liberty or Death', *The Guardian*, March 8 1995, p. 5.

4. The Society of Friends was a very well organised pressure group in its own defence at the end of the seventeenth century. Is it any the less important to defend the rights of others than our own?

I am aware that some Friends have a very negative view of pressure groups. The 'Current Trends' group that emerged in reaction to the 1987 Poverty Statement provided a platform for Friends with a distaste for the language of politics and pressure. Taunton Meeting's contribution to *Holding a Mirror* (see chapter 5, note 10) includes: 'Yearly Meeting ... is used quite unscrupulously as a platform by pressure groups: granting the

Swarthmore Lecture to the feminists was strongly deprecated, and we condemn without reservation the apparent penetration of our Society by political activists.' I trust Friends will be open to examining afresh the conditions under which BYM should use its influence.

5. Leslie J. Griffiths, 'On this issue the Church should be ablaze with anger', *The Methodist Recorder*, December 8th 1994.